BEYOND PROFESSION

THEOLOGICAL EDUCATION BETWEEN THE TIMES

Ted A. Smith, series editor

Theological Education between the Times gathers diverse groups of people for critical, theological conversations about the meanings and purposes of theological education in a time of deep change. The project is funded by the Lilly Endowment Inc.

Daniel O. Aleshire
Beyond Profession: The Next Future of Theological Education

Willie James Jennings
After Whiteness: An Education in Belonging

Mark D. Jordan
Transforming Fire: Imagining Christian Teaching

Chloe T. Sun
Attempt Great Things for God: Theological Education in Diaspora

Amos Yong
Renewing the Church by the Spirit: Theological Education after Pentecost

BEYOND PROFESSION

The Next Future of Theological Education

Daniel O. Aleshire

WILLIAM B. EERDMANS PUBLISHING COMPANY

GRAND RAPIDS, MICHIGAN

Wm. B. Eerdmans Publishing Co.
4035 Park East Court SE, Grand Rapids, Michigan 49546
www.eerdmans.com

27 26 25 24 23 22 21   1 2 3 4 5 6 7

ISBN 978-0-8028-7875-5

Library of Congress Cataloging-in-Publication Data

Names: Aleshire, Daniel O., 1947– author.
Title: Beyond profession : the next future of theological education /
    Daniel O. Aleshire.
Description: Grand Rapids, Michigan : William B. Eerdmans Publish-
    ing Company, 2021. | Series: Theological education between the
    times | Includes bibliographical references. | Summary: "A reflec-
    tion on the historical evolution of American theological education
    and its possible future development focused on formation"—
    Provided by publisher.
Identifiers: LCCN 2020042329 | ISBN 9780802878755
Subjects: LCSH: Theology—Study and teaching—United
    States—History.
Classification: LCC BV4030 .A738 2021 | DDC 230.071/173—dc23
LC record available at https://lccn.loc.gov/2020042329

Contents

Gratitude

This book reflects the help, support, and instruction of many, and I want to express my deep gratitude to them.

Ted Smith has led the Theological Education between the Times project with insight and generosity and made thoughtful suggestions throughout the development of this manuscript. Rachelle Green, Ulrike Guthrie, and the senior fellows of this project provided a wonderful community of conversation about theological education that nurtured my thoughts in more ways than I can express. I am grateful for the comments that Keri Day, Katerina Schuth, OSF, Glenn Miller, and Bill J. Leonard made to early drafts of the second chapter. Jeremiah McCarthy, Chloe Sun, Mark Jordan, and David L. Tiede read the entire manuscript and contributed significantly to its improvement.

I have had the privilege of working with the presidents and deans of the schools that comprise the Association of Theological Schools in the United States and Canada for almost three decades. They have shared the struggles, successes, and stories of their institutions with me and, in so doing, have taught me most of what I know about theological education.

I mention in the first chapter that it had been fifty years since I started seminary. I married during seminary years, and my wife and I celebrated our fiftieth wedding anniversary as this manuscript came to its conclusion. Her intellectual and personal gifts are both exquisite and bountiful. Thank you, Jo.

Prelude

I imagine that most of you reading this paragraph are busy working in some form of theological education, but that none of you has theological education for an academic area. You are more in need of something to scan than something to read. And that is okay. I spent a career on planes, in meetings, making speeches, writing proposals, talking with funders, attending to students in a seminary, and administering an organization. Time for reading was rare. I read about theological education whenever I could, but my bookshelf accumulated more "you-should-read-this" books than I care to admit.

This book is really an extended essay, but since some of you might need credit with others for reading books, we will call it a book. It is about the next future of theological education. There have already been many futures, at various times and in various cultural and religious contexts, and the next future will not be the last one. Because I cannot say for sure what the next one *will* be, I focus on what it *should* be.

The first chapter reflects on my own theological education, an education that has shaped my career and informs my hunches about the future. Theological education as I received it as a student, taught in it as a professor, and accredited it as executive director of the Association of Theological Schools can be characterized as postbaccalaureate education for religious leaders and others pursuing theological studies with a theological cur-

1

riculum that includes several theological disciplines. It entails instruction that is oriented primarily to the educational goals of knowledge and competence and is characterized by educational practices typical of degree-granting schools. This kind of theological education is located in theological schools that are accountable to standards of quality in higher education. Each of these descriptors has a story, and each is contested.

The second chapter reviews the history that has brought theological education to its present forms and practices. By my reading, three factors have shaped the development of theological education since colonial days—religion, culture, and higher education—and I argue that they will likely influence theological education in the future. This chapter is longer than the others, for reasons that I will explain, and it is one that I find fascinating because theological schools embody and extend religious movements and cultural moments. I took church history in seminary, but I learned it at a new level, one seminary at a time, as I discovered how each was an artifact of some religious impulse, some longing, some hope for the way a Christian-formed community might find its way in the world.

The third chapter describes what I think should be the next dominant model of theological education—what I call formational theological education. This kind of education is not a complete departure from the current model but accents different elements and shifts the focus. "Formation" is a term that is now widely used, even though it was contested while I was working in theological education. It is particularly useful precisely because it is undefined, and I try to articulate in this chapter what formational theological education is all about.

The fourth chapter explores the educational practices that such formational theological education will require. In this chapter I confess that I have never been the kind of educator who gets excited about educational process. What I have learned over the years, however, is that an educational idea is disembodied without a pedagogical reference. An educational strategy completes the definition of an educational idea, and in a faith where even

God takes on flesh, it is religiously necessary to think about the educational practices that embody an educational idea. So, the final chapter describes a range of practices that formational theological education will require.

That's the book! I asked a friend to read a draft of this book on a flight from Dallas to Boston, and he did. So, this book is one long airplane ride of reading. I imagine busy seminary administrators doing the same. I hope you will get a diet soft drink or glass of wine, whichever the piety of your tradition encourages, settle back in a seat that cannot be made comfortable, and give it a read.

1

Time and Change, Church and Theological Education

> We live in time—it holds us and molds us—
> but I never felt I understood it very well.
> And I'm not referring to theories about how
> it bends and doubles back, or may exist
> elsewhere in parallel versions. No, I mean
> ordinary, everyday time, which clocks and
> watches assure us passes regularly: tick-tock,
> click-clock. Is there anything more plausible
> than a second hand? And yet it takes only the
> smallest pleasure or pain to teach us time's
> malleability. Some emotions speed it up, oth-
> ers slow it down; occasionally, it seems to go
> missing—until the eventual point when it
> really does go missing, never to return.
>
> —*Julian Barnes,*
> The Sense of an Ending

The editor of a university press spoke to a group of theological educators who had won research grants in a competition sponsored by the Association of Theological Schools. He showed them a cartoon depicting a huge desk with a thick manuscript sitting on it titled *A Tale of Two Cities*. Behind the desk was a large man; in front of it was a diminutive man in Victorian dress. The caption read: "Mr. Dickens, it is either the best of times or the worst of times. It cannot be both."

It is not clear to me if Dickens was right and these are indeed both the best of times and the worst of times in American theological education, nor is it clear that the editor was right that these must be either the best of times or the worst of times. What is clear is that these are complex times with an abundance of threats and opportunities that demand new forms and challenges to retain legacies, with new schools being founded as old ones are merging or closing.

These issues are not unique to theological education. Exchange "American Christianity" for "American theological education" in the paragraph above, and it would be equally true. American theological schools are intimately tied to American communities of faith. If schools have a problem finding students, the church is as much a part of the issue as the seminary recruitment office. If congregations are failing, the seminary is as much a part of the issue as the congregation's social context or membership. It is a complex time for both American Christianity and theological education. It is the best of times for some parts of both and the worst of times for other parts.

Recently, I participated in a conference call with a consultant assessing what should influence a theological school planning for the future. Several of the participants worked primarily with pastors and congregations. They said that the future needs pastors who are more culturally and congregationally literate. The standardizing influences on congregations—like denominational patterns of work—have waned. Congregations are increasingly different from one another and thus in need of leaders who can understand this uniqueness and guide them skillfully into the future. A pastor I respect a great deal forwarded to me a copy of a letter he had recently sent to the dean of the theological school he had graduated from decades earlier. This pastor leads a congregation in a major American city that has been at the forefront on issues of racial inclusion, has cultivated a voice on social justice issues, and has developed a range of ministries for those in need. The congregation has an outsized influence in its city. This pastor expressed his gratitude to the dean for the theological education he had received, but with this concern: "there was no direct intention of instructing me on how to be a deeply centered spiritual person. How can I lead a congregation without learning the deep, spiritual practices?" What is needed in the increasing complexity of leading an American congregation—an expanded repertoire of professional skills or more intense cultivation of Christian spirituality?

It is the worst of times; it is the best of times; it is a complex time; it is a time to slow down and re-vision; it is a time to catch up to the pace of change; it is a troubling time; it is a time like every other time; it is a unique time. Time and change are woven together. A congregation that never changes has no future. A congregation that is always changing has no past. Change and time are not only institutional realities, they are also personal ones. This book constitutes what I want to say about American theological education at the conclusion of the four decades I have been involved in it. Time and change are the primary markers of these decades, and recounting these years sets the stage for thinking about what may come next. It is a future of which I am confident, even if it is one I will never see.

I entered seminary in 1969 and thought I knew what time it was. It was a socially turbulent time—civil rights struggle and the Vietnam War, strained social institutions, competing norms for sexual expression, changing gender roles, and the onslaught of the first of the boomers ready to influence society. It was a time that could be told. Religious institutions were facing changes but had robust structures to handle them. Many people were asking about the role of the church in a morally conflicted time; some were asking whether God was dead; but few were asking whether the church would die. I knew that time was moving forward, that it didn't wait, and I thought that it was on my side. I knew things were a-changin', and I imagined they were changing in positive ways.

A decade later, in 1979, I was completing my first year as a seminary professor. Many social structures had become less secure, or at least less sure of themselves. Churches and ecclesial structures, though still robust, were nonetheless changing, but not along the trajectories that had been presumed in earlier decades. Mainline Protestant churches were declining in membership although continuing as a social presence. The culture still paid deference to religion. The reforms of Vatican II had changed many practices of the Catholic Church—an institution that has a way of perceiving itself as outside of history and therefore outside of time. Evangelical Protestants had emerged from separatist and fundamentalist pasts and, along with new movements that had never been part of those pasts, were becoming more influential. Some evangelicals created new forms of religious expression, and others created new forces in American politics. More of the new was coming from less of the old; discontinuity was becoming the most continuous reality. It was still possible to tell the time, but while some changes were positive, others seemed foreboding.

Still another decade later, in 1989, I was appointed to the staff of the Association of Theological Schools (ATS). I began to administer its accrediting function the following year. I spent most of the next three decades working with the association and its member schools. Over these decades, theological education changed—perceptibly, even palpably—as did denominations, religious practices, and higher education. Denominations weakened as ecclesial structures and the loyalty of church attenders to their denominations weakened even more. Religious practices morphed, expanded, and took on altogether new forms. Evangelical Protestants became the dominant Protestant presence. The percentage of Americans who claimed a religious preference decreased, and "no religious preference" became the fastest-growing religious category. The Roman Catholic Church in the United States moved significantly toward becoming majority Hispanic. Higher education changed, and perhaps for the first time in American history, it began to lose its cultural luster. Student indebtedness increased, questions intensified as the economic value of college degrees became increasingly debatable, and public suspicions about the contribution of colleges and universities to a cultural good increased. Theological schools, deeply influenced both by ecclesial structures and by higher education, were rattled. The number and kinds of theological schools changed. While many new schools were founded, some old schools closed or merged with other institutions. New religious and ethnic constituencies gained numeric strength as others declined, and correspondingly, the number of students from minoritized racial and ethnic groups increased while the number of white students decreased. The enrollment in the master of divinity—the traditional degree for ordination—decreased, while enrollment in other professional master's programs increased.

This book was finished in 2019, fifty years after I entered seminary and forty years after theological education became my life's work. The decades have passed swiftly, and the changes have been many. Some of them have been exhilarating, others heartbreaking. I concluded my work at ATS deeply aware that the fabric of time and change can be holy and hopeful as well as dizzying and dismal.

While historians have generally been able to name broad intellectual moments, the name most often used for the current period is "postmodern," as if the present moment, though different from the last one, does not yet have enough identity for its own distinct name. It is as if we are between the times—the name given to the series of books about theological education of which this book is a part. If we were sure about the time (even if it were the worst of times!), it might be easier to project the future, but we have the time that we have, whatever time it is. Older systems seem to be growing less useful, while the most recent inventions seem less than adequate.

This between-the-times time has generated anxiety in theological education. Money is harder to find. The kind of education that once attracted students to leave home and relocate to new intellectual worlds has less power to attract. The current moment has invented new educational strategies that make it possible for many students to stay at home, turn on their computers, and accumulate religious knowledge. Where is theological education going? What is the future of theological education? There have already been many futures, as Justo L. González has shown.[1] What will the next one be? Will the next theological education be as good for its time as previous expressions have been for theirs? It is not clear to me that what it should be is what it will be. But time has a way of pushing toward what can be and compressing it into what should be. The name of this process is hope—not because history inevitably pushes toward improvement or betterment, but because God beckons and pulls all creation in the direction of God's own purposes.

A Personal Theological Education

In the mid-1980s I was following two soon-to-be seminary graduates on their walk to the chapel for a rehearsal for the commencement service. They were midcareer students, which was less common then than it is now. As I eavesdropped on their conversation, I heard one say to the other, "I'm going to miss this place like I miss Vietnam." I had not had either for a course, and if I had, I am confident it would not have changed their assessment. Seminary does not work for everyone, but I think that it did work for me. Given the occasional fuzziness of my memory, it surprises me how vivid some recollections from my seminary days are.

The socially turbulent years of the civil rights struggle and the Vietnam War were an interesting time to be in seminary. Protests were increasingly intense as the nation grew ever more war weary. Following the shooting of student protestors at Kent State University, the seminary I attended designated a day of prayer. One class I had that semester was led by a professor we regarded as especially wise. He came to the lectern, and after a moment of silence said, as best I remember: "My namesake (the son of another professor) is in Sweden because he could not participate in this war. My own son is in the Mekong Delta today. You tell me how to pray." With that, he left the room. Students sat in silence for a time, then left quietly, one by one. That moment remains profoundly powerful for me. What does it mean to pray? How do we know what our most earnest petitions should be?

I grew up in a pietistic tradition that valued the importance of devotional aspects of the Christian life but had limited perspective on the long tradition of Christian spirituality or the classic devotional literature. In a course on the classics of Christian devotion one semester, I read Saint John of the Cross and Saint Teresa of Ávila, Thomas Merton and Dorothy Day, John Woolman and Thomas Kelly, Dietrich Bonhoeffer and Alfred Delp, John Bunyan and Dag Hammarskjöld, and many more. I think it was the most reading that I ever did for a single course. By the end of the semester, I had a history, a literature, and a theology that constituted a more nuanced understanding of Christian spirituality. The literature has stayed with me, and the books that I read that semester have an honored place on my bookshelves. The witness and struggles of the saints have stayed with me these ensuing decades.

Then there was a course on the teaching of Jesus. The reading list was extensive, including Rudolf Bultmann's *Jesus and the Word*. The problems with Bultmann's work have been the subject of scholarly attention since the 1970s, but passages in that book grabbed me and have not let go. "The Kingdom of God is not an ideal which realizes itself in human history; . . . we can say only that it draws near, it comes, it appears."[2] Reading that book and paying attention to the content of that class changed how I understood the future toward which Christians are called.

These experiences became part of the lens through which I have viewed ministry. It is still not altogether clear to me why these experiences continue to be so vivid, why I remember them while many others have been forgotten, or perhaps more importantly, what the nature of theological learning really is. I earned a master of divinity—a ninety-hour postbaccalaureate degree. Roughly a third of the curriculum was devoted to Scripture and biblical languages; a third to theology, history, and ethics; and a third to courses in pastoral studies. Most MDiv degrees have fewer hours now, but the percentages across these three broad areas are likely similar. I doubt if any current reading lists for courses in ATS member schools include any of the books

I read, except for some of the classic devotional and theological texts. While there are differences today, there is enough continuity that my memories inform what is of value in today's theological education, and, having observed a career's worth of changes, I have some hunches about theological education in the coming decades.

Learning in the Christian Tradition

My first idea about theological education formed long before I ever took a seminary class. It came from the inscription in the flyleaf of the Bible my parents gave me as a Christmas present when I was in the fifth or sixth grade. It was a study Bible; my parents had determined that I needed to move from a Bible with pictures to one with notes and cross-references. The inscription in my father's hand referred to 2 Timothy 2:15, "Study to shew thyself approved unto God, a workman that needeth not to be ashamed, rightly dividing the word of truth" (KJV). I read this Bible all the way through during my high school years. I now have contrary positions to almost all its notes and interpretations, as well as its dating of events. I have a different idea of who may have written 2 Timothy and what it means to "rightly divide" the word. The importance of study, however, remains unshakable.

The Christian tradition gives study a prominent place. Maybe it is because Jesus was a teacher, maybe it is because of the often indirect way that Jesus taught with parables, maybe it is because Christianity emerged from Judaism with its highly cultivated role for teaching, maybe it is because of the intellectual capacity of Paul as Christianity's earliest interpreter, maybe it is because of the function of religion that makes meaning and interprets reality—whatever the reason is, study has been central to Christian practices. Learning informs and, in its most successful moments, transforms. If theological education were eliminated before anyone reads this book, it would reemerge quickly because learning is intrinsic to the Christian faith. Learning, however, is not without its problems. It raises as many questions as it provides answers.

One of the problems is embedded in what I think my father meant by learning as an act of faith. On the one hand, he prompted me to attend to the importance of study, but on the other, he had a qualified perception of the value of learning: a certain kind of learning was good, but another kind was suspect. Learning that justified what one's group believed was good, but learning that challenged faith was questionable. That was not just his idea: never during my years as a seminary professor was there a time when some students did not tell me they had been cautioned that seminary could ruin their faith. One is "approved unto God" by study that "rightly divides the word," and for some people the only way the word is "rightly divided" is when it confirms what they already believe. By this perspective, the wrong kind of learning can be as detrimental to faith as the right kind can be beneficial.

Learning, especially its most advanced forms, generates complexity. When Paul makes his famous statement of faith to King Agrippa, Festus exclaims: "You are out of your mind, Paul! Too much learning is driving you insane!" (Acts 26:24).[3] Festus was not right about Paul's sanity, but he was right about a consequence of learning: it problematizes; it confuses. Learning invites the examination of an issue from many sides. The accrual of reliable information often points toward multiple interpretations rather than clarifying a single point of view. It is, for example, easier to believe one concept of creation when one is not confronted with two accounts in Genesis that have a certain tension between them. It is easier to have one view of marriage from the creation account if one does not study carefully other patterns of marriage that go without condemnation in the Scripture—from Solomon's practice of polygamy to Paul's advocacy of celibacy. Learning complicates believing, and if the greatest Christian virtue is to be "absolutely sure" of something, then learning is not necessarily a friend of faith. The preacher of Ecclesiastes is right:

CHAPTER 1

For in much wisdom is much vexation,
and those who increase knowledge increase sorrow.

(Eccles. 1:18)

It is one thing to be cautious about learning, it is another to oppose it altogether. Some Christians have argued that, while learning is a human activity that may benefit some areas of human engagement, it is of limited consequence to the life of faith. The Spirit will give the gifts necessary to accomplish God's goals for creation and redemption, they say. Learning, in this view of God's action, is an act of unfaith, not a discipline of faith. For people to do a great thing without learning is a sign of God's blessing. To sing beautifully without training and to preach movingly without education are signs that God, and not human effort, is the author of the singing and preaching. From this perspective, knowledge without learning affirms that God is above all and gives the gifts necessary to accomplish God's purposes. The Jews, who are never treated pleasantly in John's Gospel, are astonished by Jesus's demonstrated knowledge and ask: "How does this man have such learning, when he has never been taught?" (John 7:15). Jewish traditions have not diminished the importance of learning as some Christians have, but the astonishment in this text is precisely the point some Christians want to make—that knowing religious truth does not necessarily come from human knowing.

Some who affirm the importance of learning question how learning occurs. Are people faithful because they have learned the right thing, or do they learn to be faithful by doing the right thing? Do people learn to do right by understanding the right and behaving accordingly, or do they learn to do right by doing it, and then figuring out in what way it was right? Is the goal of learning in a theological school primarily gaining biblical and theological knowledge or is it learning a Christian way of being in the world? To value learning as an act of faith does not settle questions about what is most important to learn and how it is learned.

Learning has its shadow side. Most references in the Bible about knowledge are positive—it is something to be desired and a resource for good—but it has another role in the garden of Eden: "of the tree of the knowledge of good and evil you shall not eat, for in the day that you eat of it you shall die" (Gen. 2:17). It is the only prohibition that God gave the human family, and disregarding the prohibition became humanity's original disobedience. Some knowledge belongs to God, and access to it is only through relationship with God. To gain this knowledge apart from God is to declare human independence from God, and knowledge split apart from God is like atoms splitting in a nuclear explosion. The power unleashed causes great damage. Knowledge, when removed from the divine source, can become idolatrous and destructive; it eviscerates the goodness of learning and its generative contribution to human flourishing.

The shadow side of learning is also evident when a good thing is used the wrong way. Jesus confronts the Pharisees with these words: "Woe to you lawyers! For you have taken away the key of knowledge; you did not enter yourselves, and you hindered those who were entering" (Luke 11:52). The text suggests that knowledge can be misused or kept away from people who could benefit from it. Knowledge has power, and anything that has power can be misused and abused. It can be God's gift when freely shared, but it can also be used to lord it over others, to think better of oneself than one ought, or to look down on others who do not know as much.

Learning has two sides, like most human activities. One side provides a key to discipleship and the leadership of communities of faith. The other side causes harm and idolatry. How does learning lean into the good that it is and away from the bad that it can do? Does knowledge have a fatal flaw as it did in the garden, or does it contribute to human flourishing and faithful leadership? Learning can lead to the very heart of mystery, but it can also transform simple obedience into artificial complexity.

I still have the Bible my parents gave me. The binding is tattered from use when I was in high school. My father's note in the flyleaf is the only thing that I have in his handwriting—he died accidentally only a few years after he had written it. I remain convinced that he was right, perhaps for reasons altogether different from the ones he had in mind. I think that study is central to Christian life, to faithful discipleship, and to effective leadership of communities of faith. When it is properly disciplined, all the good it can do is multiplied and all the bad is diminished. Theological education is about individuals learning in a disciplined way on behalf of the communities of faith they will serve.

Contemporary Theological Education and the Arguments It Generates

Learning is the quintessential activity of the enterprise that is theological education. Theological education entails the learning children do in a Sunday school class, youth do in a confirmation class or during a mission trip, or adults do in a class on Sunday morning. It includes the learning of part-time pastors in nondegree programs and college students taking a course in Bible or theology. I have taught classes in all these settings and have witnessed the learning that can occur in each of them.

While good theological education occurs in all these settings, this book is about a particular expression of theological education: (1) *postbaccalaureate education for religious leaders and others pursuing theological studies* that (2) *offers a theological curriculum including a range of theological disciplines*, (3) *is oriented to educational goals of knowledge and competence*, and (4) *is characterized by educational practices of degree-granting schools and accountable to standards of quality in higher education.* This is the kind of theological education that I received and in which I worked for many decades. While it was assumed to be a good and viable form of theological education, it has come under increasing suspicion. Disputes abound about the level of education that learning for ministry requires; about who the students should be; about what the subjects of study should be; about the educational practices that are most appropriate and effective;

about the aims, purposes, and goals of the educational efforts; about the nature and necessity of schools as places where education occurs; and about how the quality of educational effort is assessed.

The remainder of this chapter briefly introduces some of these contests. Volumes have been written about most of them, and assessments vary by religious tradition, by prevailing intellectual paradigms, by denominational perspectives, and by higher education practices. Though space does not permit an exegesis of each of the many arguments, it is sufficient to identify some of these contests and to note how they shape perceptions about the purposes and forms that theological education should take in the future.

Postbaccalaureate Education for Religious Leaders and Others Pursuing Theological Studies

Theological education in the Christian tradition involves all the education needed to grow in Christian understanding and live out one's baptismal faith. While learning for faith is a general expectation of all Christians, the definition I have proposed focuses on graduate professional or graduate academic degree programs. This narrows theological education to religious leaders and students of theological disciplines willing and able to invest time and effort in graduate education.

Should theological education be focused primarily on religious leaders? If the Christian tradition is diminished when people neither know their faith nor accept responsibility for learning it, then theological learning should be for all. The purpose of the narrowed audience in the definition is that, in addition to the general learning for which all Christians are responsible, religious leaders have additional responsibility to learn the arts of ministry by which leadership is exercised and to learn the tradition so well that they can readily teach it to others. If the particular form of theological education that has been described is for religious leaders, then other questions emerge. For example,

narrowing theological education to religious leaders can trun-
cate a broad and long intellectual religious history in order to free
up curricular space for subjects related to the more transitory
issues of professional skills and practice. This argument gets to
the heart of a question about the ultimate purpose of theological education: Is it primarily about equipping professionals for
socially defined ministerial practice, or is it about acquiring a
theological understanding that orders life and thought as the
basis for ministerial work as well as Christian life?

Throughout this book, the focus on religious leaders will be
narrowed down—to congregational and parish leadership. It often
will be evident that when I write of religious leaders, I am thinking
primarily about the people who fill compensated roles in congregations and parishes. Many theological schools have broadened
their educational focus to faith-informed leadership in a variety
of human service roles, and more will do so in the future. Some
projections suggest that, by the mid-2020s, persons seeking the
master of divinity (MDiv), which is typically pursued for ordination,
will be fewer than those enrolled in other professional and academic master's degree programs, which are typically not related to
ordination. The backbone of both kinds of degrees, however, is a
theological curriculum that has developed for ministry conceived
as some form of pastoral service. While the narrowed focus of the
congregational context is not the only focus in theological schools,
it is the reference point used throughout this book.

If it is accepted that this kind of theological education should
be focused on religious leaders, does this kind of learning require graduate level instruction? A person once asked me what
the difference was between a baccalaureate funeral and a postbaccalaureate funeral. It was a good question. Graduate theological education consumes time and resources. By what metric
can it be concluded that this time and these resources add the
kind of value that justifies the effort and cost? The ATS voted to
begin accrediting theological schools in the 1930s for many reasons, but one was to push all schools toward postbaccalaureate
degrees, which more academically advanced schools had already

begun to offer. It worked, and graduate professional education became the norm. The rationale for the initial effort included arguments about the need for more education and for a level of education that would fit the social location and needs of religion in American society. And while the association adopted recommendations for the kind of undergraduate studies that should precede seminary studies, the case was never made that the disciplines taught in the theological school could only be learned at a postbaccalaureate level.

The assumption that they should be taught at the graduate level has come under pressure in the twenty-first century for two reasons. The first is that theological education is not as well subsidized as it has been in the past, and the cost of graduate degrees increasingly is borne by students who incur debt to pay for it. Repaying that debt can be burdensome on both seminary graduates and the small congregations they frequently serve right after graduation. The second reason is that the educational case for graduate-level degrees is best based on the assumption that students require some basic knowledge that prepares them for more advanced studies. For theological studies, that prior knowledge was assumed to be the liberal arts. In the 2018–2019 academic year, however, fewer than half of the students in master's level programs in ATS schools had educational backgrounds in the liberal arts. Can the education that is needed at the advanced level be learned without the prior knowledge? And can it be learned in fewer years? Will the future of theological education for ministry depend on graduate degrees as a normative educational requirement? In the minds of many, the question is more philosophical: *Should* education for ministry depend on graduate degrees?

Curriculum and Goals

The ATS requires accredited schools to include instruction in four broad areas for the master of divinity, a general theological degree most typically but not always oriented toward ordination. These areas include (1) religious heritage—studies that provide a comprehensive and discriminating understanding of Scripture and the historical development and contemporary articulation of a doctrinal and theological tradition; (2) community context—studies that provide a critical understanding of and creative engagement with the cultural realities and structures within which the church lives and carries out its mission in communities and globally; (3) personal and spiritual formation—learning that helps students grow in personal faith, emotional maturity, and moral integrity; and (4) capacity for ministerial and public leadership—studies and supervised experience in ministry required for leadership of communities of faith and their engagement in their communities.[4]

This curriculum has accumulated over the history of American theological education, and each major shift invited some contestation. In the nineteenth century, the study of Scripture, theology, and history was dominant, but the strategies for the scholarly study of Scripture changed, and that generated great controversy. The twentieth century introduced the disciplines associated with ministry practice and community context, and that addition was contested because it diminished the space that the "real" or "classical" subjects held in the curriculum. In the late twentieth century, some schools began giving explicit educational attention to personal and spiritual formation, although that focus had been assumed in the way Bible and theology were taught in the earliest versions of ministerial education. The introduction of curricular attention to personal and spiritual formation was contested because it was not considered the proper work of graduate schools or because the schools did not have the educational practices that this addition would require. The theological curriculum has grown over two centuries, and while substantive changes have been few, they were contested as they were introduced. The curriculum has been the context for one contest after another. It still is.

The theological curriculum is a way of ordering instruction and learning toward educational goals. Yet until the last part of the twentieth century, theological educators assumed their goals more than they articulated them. I don't remember a course syllabus from my seminary days that listed specific learning goals. My hunch is that my professors thought that students should graduate with academic knowledge about Bible, theology, church history, philosophy, ethics, and other subjects that would provide an intellectual foundation for work in ministry, and have at least a beginner's level competence in the exercise of professional skills like pastoral care, church administration, preaching, and leadership. These goals—the intellectual knowledge and pastoral skills that would support the work of ministry—defined a mature professional model of theological education.

Education, at least the best of it, results in more than the attainment of stated or assumed goals. When I think back on courses that influenced me a great deal, it seems obvious that my New Testament professor wanted students to know the Gospels' accounts of the teaching of Jesus as well as the wide range and long history of interpretation that have accrued to that teaching. He would be pleased to know that the readings in that course provided a ministry-shaping perspective for me, but I doubt if he assigned Bultmann for that reason. On that day of prayer after the Kent State shootings, I think my professor was honestly saying something about his own ambivalence about how to pray, but I doubt if he intended it to have the lasting influence on my perception of humility and prayer that it did. I make sense of these layers of intention and influence with the help of Eliot Eisner's threefold categorization of curriculum.[5] Eisner distinguishes between the explicit curriculum (what is taught toward stated goals); the null curriculum (the lesson taught by what is omitted either unintentionally or on purpose); and the hidden curriculum (the unintended kind of learning like I experienced in those two classes). Theological schools, of course, have all three, and all of them influence theological learning.

Educational Practices

The focus of theological education is students' learning more than professors' teaching, but good educational practices en-

hance the quality of learning. Over the past century, four pedagogical patterns developed in theological education, and each
pattern brought both innovation and resistance.

In the late nineteenth and early twentieth century, recitation was a dominant educational practice. My father-in-law attended the same seminary in the late 1930s that I attended in
the late 1960s. He talked more than once about his recitation-
based courses. Recitation was a pedagogical practice in many
theological schools in which students were responsible for
reading a textbook before each class session and being ready
to recite—by summary and sometimes by memory—when the
professor asked a question. The professor would then comment
on the material.

By the time I entered seminary thirty years later, the pedagogy had changed. All my professors lectured in their classes.
The lecture method made it possible for professors to present
material using their own expertise and provided a way to combine information and evaluation that reflected their own commitments. I took very few courses that followed one textbook.
Most used a variety of books and readings from which professors
drew their lectures or to which professors wanted us students to
pay particular attention. Lecturing, of course, had been a pedagogical practice for centuries, but lectures were more typically
occasional rather than a regular approach to classroom learning. I learned later that my father-in-law's professors greeted the
lecture method with suspicion. Lectures are a wonderful educational practice for professors who are gifted communicators and
can assemble the material and the arguments that are central to
evaluating different positions, but they can be tedious and bor-
ing with a less able communicator or one who presents material
orally that could be learned more efficiently through reading.

When I was a seminary professor, the lecture was still the
dominant instructional practice, but another pedagogical strategy was developing: the seminar or discussion format. This
method depends on students doing research and presenting it
to the class, or on students reading common sources and being

prepared to discuss them. Whether built on individual academic papers, group projects, or other student-focused activities, this pedagogical practice hoped to increase student learning by making the classroom more student centered. This practice, like the others, had its critics. Some of my colleagues embraced it, others used it sparingly, still others, not at all. The primary concern, of both professors and students, was that the professor, who should know the subject better than any of the students, is placed in the role of facilitating conversation and interaction and, as appropriate, correcting and expanding what students present. The net benefit of the seminar model depends on how well a professor can facilitate and comment on the discussion, how good the students are at conveying ideas and information, and how attentive students are to other students.

The most recent innovation in teaching is distance education, which has emerged along with advances in technology. This kind of education is conducted with minimal place-based interaction between faculty and students or among students. Course materials, lectures, discussions, and student-teacher interactions are conducted electronically. Library resources, for the most part, are drawn from the increasingly abundant electronic holdings in theological libraries. When this instructional model was introduced in theological education, the applications tended to "convert" a face-to-face course into a distance-learning course, which did not prove to be very effective. Over time, as theological schools have invested in faculty development and technological resources, they have revised distance-learning courses to maximize the educational strengths of online instruction, and another pedagogical strategy was invented. These practices have, in many contexts, also resulted in revised strategies for on-campus courses. Like the other innovations in teaching and instructional practices, this one has been greeted with suspicion—perhaps even more so than the others. The primary concern is that spiritual and intellectual formation occurs most readily in the contexts of community and interpersonal interactions, and distance-education strategies minimize these opportunities. Another concern is the effectiveness of distance-education models for teaching the skills of ministry like preaching, teaching, and pastoral care. Even in the face of these concerns, distance-education courses have become common, and in the 2017–2018 and 2018–2019 academic years, before the pandemic forced all schools to adopt the strategy in 2020, almost 40 percent of all students enrolled in ATS member schools completed at least one course in this format.

The development of teaching strategies in theological education has tended to follow developments that occurred more broadly in higher education. Yet, in every case, theological schools embraced these strategies later than did higher education in general, and with more suspicion. Theological schools tend to be educationally conservative. Most are also small institutions with limited resources to develop and embrace new educational models. They have, however, been dragged to adopt each of these educational inventions—usually kicking and screaming—and each has contributed new forms of engagement, accommodated different learning styles and student needs, and in the case of distance-learning innovations, increased access to students.

Theological Schools

Schools have changed over time, but *school* has been the dominant location for theological education. In the colonial era, theological education took place in colleges, some of which became universities with divinity schools, but in the nineteenth century, freestanding theological schools became the dominant setting for both Roman Catholic and Protestant theological education. When I began work at ATS, more than 80 percent of all schools educating ministers and priests were freestanding educational institutions. They provided a common space for teachers with knowledge, a library with books, and students with a desire, if not the requirement, to study. Like all schools, they provided a context in which learning could occur in classrooms, libraries, chapels, and refectories. Through the first half of the twentieth century, and into the second, few people questioned whether a "school" was a good place to conduct theological education. If anything, the assumption was that no other place would be as acceptable. Like everything else in the past fifty years, this assumption came under review, and questions emerged.

The concerns are many. One is that a school may not be a good setting for all the kinds of learning that theological education requires. A school, with its classrooms and courses, is an ideal location for learning subjects like Bible, theology, history, philosophy, and other disciplines that utilize academic practices like reading books, listening to lectures, engaging in discussions, and writing papers. It is less adept, however, at providing the kind of educational space in which advanced skills in ministry can be learned. Does a student learn to preach well by hearing lectures about preaching and sacred rhetoric and then preaching in front of a professor and other students, or by preaching in the context of communities gathered for worship? Another concern is that the seminary can become a hothouse more than a seedbed. Schools can provide a totalizing environment in which students learn to be clergy but, in the process, become separated from the very people—anyone not clergy—they should understand intimately and with whom they will work collaboratively in parishes and congregations. A good school provides support structures and academic engagement with theological studies that will be absent in the settings in which graduates will serve, and the very nature of a school may impede preparation for the work they will do. Also troubling is that, in this century, the cost of running a freestanding graduate school has increased significantly. The indirect expenses for many freestanding schools—the cost of the business office, president's office, institutional advancement, facilities maintenance and support, and technology—are greater than the direct expenses of faculty salaries, academic administration, and library. As a result, many freestanding schools are affiliating with larger educational institutions, and new schools are typically being founded in such settings. While 20 percent of ATS member schools were units of a college or university in

1990, about 40 percent are now affiliated with larger educational institutions.

Since the 1980s, theological schools have expanded the location of education so that students could attend seminary without *going* to seminary—without relocating in order to attend. The result is that "school" is not as prevalent an institution for theological education as it once was. The phenomenon of "school" has been morphing from a location with a prescribed set of activities to a prescribed set of activities in many "locations," or in the case of distance education, in no institutional location at all. Face-to-face theological education on a seminary campus remains the dominant pattern in America, but it is not the only pattern, and school as an institution in one location is far less central to theological education in the twenty-first century than it was in most of the twentieth century.

Accountable to Standards of Quality in Higher Education

Schools are not all the same. Some are judged to be better than others, and over the past century the criteria by which that judgment is made have changed. The quality of theological schools is often determined by criteria similar to those used to determine quality in other institutions of higher education, and those criteria changed during the twentieth century.

At the beginning of the century, the dominant criteria for determining quality were the resources of the school. The "best" schools had the following: faculty members educated in the most elite graduate programs and who published significant research, endowments or other financial resources of significant size, students who had graduated from the best undergraduate programs, an excellent library, and beautiful and spacious facilities. Many decisions about the quality of schools continue to be made on the basis of these criteria. However, after World War II, as higher education institutions became increasingly diverse, schools began to be judged by correlating the fiscal, library, faculty training, and competencies of faculty with the mission of the institution. A community college focused on teaching, for example, does not need the same size or kind of library or research productivity of faculty as a school that offers a research doctorate. A community college can be a very good community college—well suited to its purposes and mission—and look very different from a research-intensive university. This pattern of determining quality makes possible different definitions of quality, depending on the mission of the institution. It allows theological schools to be judged as theological schools and not as liberal arts colleges or research universities, even though they possess certain elements of both. A third way to judge the quality of a school is by the outcomes of its work. By this model, quality should be determined by the extent to which a school's graduates have attained its stated learning outcomes. The best schools are the ones whose educational goals are achieved, quite apart from how much money they have or how beautiful their facilities might be. This pattern became dominant in the late twentieth century, and schools have worked hard to develop the capacities to assess learning that it requires.

These three ways of determining quality have emerged in three historic moments over a century, and they tend to function cumulatively. The national mood in the United States, however, with its increasing insistence that higher education justify its cost by demonstrating the employability, productivity, and earnings of graduates, has placed a disproportionate focus on particular outcomes that may not be the most important for higher education. Each of these patterns of determining quality has its problems, but they are the patterns to which theological schools, as graduate professional institutions, are accountable.

When I think about the elements in this definition of theological education, the arguments they have generated, and the changes they reflect, it strikes me how much has happened during the years I have worked in theological education. I worked as a professor with two of the three dominant pedagogical strategies that were mentioned. During my years with the accrediting agency, I dealt with two of the three models of judging quality in higher education. I was educated in the graduate professional model; I taught and administered in that model; and in the last decade I have begun to see how that model was becoming inadequate. In short, I have not only reported on the contests that these changes have elicited but I have experienced them. In the fifty years I have been a student, researcher, professor, and administrator in theological education, I have witnessed a settled system become stressed in almost every way that it was settled when I entered seminary in 1969. Why are *all* these elements of theological education experiencing stress *now*? Why have fifty years brought so many uncontested assumptions about theological education into question? Has time gone missing? Are the present cultural forces, changing religious practices, and questions about higher education creating a force field that is bending theological education into new shapes? Will the current debates result in revised, coherent, and agreed-upon patterns of theological education in the future? The remainder of this extended essay addresses these questions.

2

Diverse Histories, Common Influences

> When does the past become the past? How much time must elapse before what merely happened begins to give off the mysterious, numinous glow that is the mark of true pastness?
>
> —*John Banville,*
> Time Pieces: A Dublin Memoir

It is not clear that the founders of most theological schools knew they were making history when they started schools, typically with frail and fledgling collections of books, a professor or two, and a few students. But these schools persisted, and founding stories invariably helped form institutional sagas. At some point, the inconsequential became old enough to be historical and acquired the ability to bestow institutional gravitas. Theological schools have been founded by immigrant communities as they became established in America, by denominations experiencing growth, by one side or another in theological struggles, by people seeking to advance a theological vision, and by denominations expanding their geographical bases. They are founded when some religious vision has energy and is perceived to have consequence, and they remain historical artifacts of that energy even after it dissipates. Most theological schools change over time, especially over long periods of time, but they carry defining marks from their founding through those changes. The past does not determine the future, but its layers of influence never go away.

While future forms and practices of theological education may not be an extension of current forms and practices, certain agents that have influenced theological schools in the past will influence their future. This essay does not have space for a comprehensive history; that would take volumes, and those histories have already been written. I want to share enough history, however, to test this hypothesis and to allow you to judge for yourself. I think theological schools have been influenced by three fundamental forces: the cultural moment, practices in higher education, and religious structures and practices. Very different kinds of schools, emerging at different times in American history, reflect these variables of influence.

This chapter is different from the others in this book in four ways. First, it is longer. I could not find a shorter way to test my hypothesis about these three influencers, and give you a chance to test my analysis, and tell the story in any less detail.

Second, it has a different voice. The first chapter tells much of the story of my life in theological education. As old as I am, however, I have no personal account of the three hundred years of theological education that preceded me, so I need to rely on the voices of others and the historians who have recorded them. I will return to a more personal voice in the other chapters.

Third, this chapter looks at theological schools in the context of mainline Protestant, Roman Catholic, and evangelical Protestant theological education. No group of schools is homogeneous, of course, and schools within each of these groups differ from one another, sometimes significantly. For the most part, however, the schools have more affinity with other schools in their group than with schools outside their group, and this organizational structure is historically instructive.

Fourth, it gives special attention to historically black schools and the presence of racial/ethnic communities in theological education. While historically black schools are certainly Protestant, they would be hidden in an analysis that includes only evangelical and mainline Protestant schools. And, because much of the future of theological schools will depend on the participation of racial/ethnic communities, they are given some attention as well.

After this chapter, I will return to a more personal voice, keep the pages fewer, and address issues of theological education in terms of all the schools and all the students, although the rest of this essay depends on issues that are explored in this chapter.

Mainline Protestant Theological Education

Much of the history of mainline Protestant theological education predates the designation of these schools as "mainline." The mainline-evangelical distinction had not emerged in colonial and nineteenth-century theological schools, although such schools contained elements of both strands.[1] With a few notable exceptions, the history of Protestant theological education from the colonial era to the early twentieth century is relegated to denominations that would now be considered mainline Protestant. It is a story that can be told in four parts: (1) education in the colonial period and the earliest years of nationhood; (2) schools that developed and matured in the nineteenth century; (3) the triumph and trauma of the first half of the twentieth century; and (4) the complexity of theological education for a divided Protestantism from the Second World War to the present moment.[2]

Colonial and Early Nationhood

Harvard College was established as the first American institution of higher education in 1636 "by vote of the Great and General Court of the Massachusetts Bay Colony and named after the College's first benefactor, John Harvard of Charlestown, a minister who upon his death in 1638 gave his library and half of his estate to the young college with a total enrollment of nine students."[3] It would be several decades before a second college was founded, in Virginia, in the 1690s, when "clergy of the Church of England in Virginia adopted at a convention 'Several Propositions' for founding a college to consist of three schools: grammar, philosophy and divinity." Three years later, "King William III and Queen Mary II granted a charter to establish The College of William and Mary in Virginia."[4] In New England, the efforts of colonial clergymen across several decades culminated in the founding of Yale in 1701, when a "charter was granted for a school 'wherein Youth may be instructed in the Arts and Sciences (and) through the blessing of Almighty God may be fitted for Publick employment both in Church and Civil State.'"[5] As the eighteenth century progressed, the College of New Jersey was founded in 1746 in Elizabeth, New Jersey, by the Presbyterian Synod for the education of ministers.

These seventeenth- and eighteenth-century schools consti-tuted the earliest expressions of higher education in North Amer-ica and were all founded by religious bodies with educational goals like Yale's: to prepare persons for employment in the church or civil state. Education for ministry was not unique. Glenn Miller writes that "clergy and laity were to receive the same education, one that fitted them ideally for service in either of the two pub-lic realms, church or commonwealth."[6] These colonial schools adapted an English college model in which education cultivated "learned gentleman," where "learned" typically meant steeped in classical subjects and languages, and "gentlemen" designated cultural elites. In England, with its established state and struc-tures, this model perpetuated the influence of elite and aristo-cratic classes. In America, by contrast, it provided the education of persons who would build a national culture. The combination of many colonies' established religions and a common education for both civic and religious service made it possible for colonial religious leaders to work in both spheres. John Witherspoon, for example, was a minister and president of the College of New Jer-sey when he signed the Declaration of Independence. This early form of theological education contributed both to the founding of educational institutions and to the building of American culture. It was an auspicious beginning for theological education, and its influence in American education and culture has likely never been greater than it was in these early years.

Of course, not all Protestant ministers were educated in these fledgling institutions. The First Great Awakening fomented emotive religious energy in the eighteenth century that garnered converts and motivated missionary efforts to the western and southern frontiers. Baptists and Methodists on the frontier often did not receive a formal theological education, either because they were unable to attend schools generally located in the east or because they thought it both unnecessary and risky, in that it replaced the warmth of revival with the coolness of reason. Their theological education was gained by apprenticing with more experienced ministers or by reading texts like those assigned by the early Methodist circuit riders, or simply by studying the Bible as they preached it. Since it was an informal system, few records exist about how many were trained this way, but it is likely that more were trained in these informal systems than in the colleges.

Nineteenth-Century and Denominational Seminaries

In the nineteenth century, the formal education for ministers gradually moved away from colleges to specialized theological schools. The education of ministers in universities like Harvard and Yale moved to separate university units that matured as divinity schools. The first freestanding Protestant seminary was Andover in Massachusetts (which became Andover Newton), founded in 1808 by Congregationalists who opposed the appointment of a Unitarian-leaning professor to the Hollis Chair at Harvard (the oldest endowed chair in American higher education). The second was Princeton Theological Seminary, founded by Presbyterians who wanted to separate ministerial education from the College of New Jersey, now Princeton University. While Andover was not under strict church control, the founding documents required every professor to be "a man of sound and orthodox principles in divinity" and to make a public declaration of his opposition not only to "Atheists and Infidels, but to Jews, Mahommetans, Arians, Pelagians, Antinomians, Socinians, Unitarians, and Universalists, and to all other heresies and errors, ancient and modern, which may be opposed to the Gospel of Christ, or hazardous to the souls of men."[7] Princeton required faculty to swear "an ex animo (literally, from the soul) oath that their theology was that of the Westminster Confession and Catechisms."[8] These freestanding theological schools were denominational in focus, if not in outright ownership and control.

The founding of freestanding seminaries resulted in two significant developments. The first was a more specialized theological curriculum. The curriculum at Andover, for example, included "natural theology" (apologetics, philosophy, and ethics), sacred literature, ecclesiastical history, and Christian theology. The second development was that theological studies, for the most part, were removed from university studies, and as a consequence, from the broader intellectual agenda that the universities pursued. Freestanding schools were part church entities and part higher education entities. They were related to but different from both, and this would become a defining characteristic in their support, growth, theological battles, and institutional struggles.

In the span of a few decades in the early nineteenth century, Congregationalists, Presbyterians, Episcopalians, Baptists, and Lutherans all had seminaries that were independent of other educational institutions and tightly related to a single denomination. The freestanding denominational seminary became the dominant institutional form for the education of ministers for the nineteenth and much of the twentieth centuries. As the form matured, so did theological disciplines, and as disciplines matured, scholarship became more specialized. The scholarly methods for the study of the Old Testament, for example, became increasingly different from the methods used in church history.

While Protestant theological schools developed institutional forms and specialized educational content after their separation from colleges and universities, they functioned much as the rest of higher education of the time did. Disciplines of study developed in colleges, universities, and freestanding theological schools in similar ways. As disciplines emerged, academic guilds were formed by faculty. What are now the Society of Biblical Literature and the American Society of Church History were founded in the 1880s—the same decade as the American Historical Association, when "history had only recently emerged as a distinct academic discipline."[9] Knowledge was expanding, the United States was becoming more urban, and theological education—like higher education more broadly—was accommodating to a changed perception of advanced learning and the growing complexity of ministry.

Protestant denominations were competitive with one another in the nineteenth century, and large social distances were created from small doctrinal differences. Denominational seminaries both reflected and contributed to the competition. For the most part, only Presbyterians taught in or went to Presbyterian seminaries, just as only Congregationalists and only Baptists taught in or went to Congregational and Baptist seminaries, respectively. The homogeneity of faculty and students in denominational schools provided contexts in which students were socialized to particular kinds of ministry in particularized denominational structures. For all the competition among denominations, however, Protestants shared an important cultural privilege in the form of a quasi-established religion. While legal establishment was forbidden by the Bill of Rights to the US Constitution, Protestantism functioned much like an established church.[10] This functional reality extended cultural privilege from denominations to the theological schools affiliated with them. The century ended with a culturally established Protestantism that was ordered by competitive, institutionally robust denominational structures. It began with two freestanding theological schools and ended with the more than fifty that survived to serve what would become mainline Protestantism in the twentieth century.

Twentieth-Century Triumph and Trauma

Protestants began the twentieth century with confidence. They established a magazine in the late nineteenth century that was renamed the *Christian Century* in 1900, a name reflecting that confidence. Several factors that had emerged in the previous century would influence Protestant theological education in the new century.

The institutional and scholarly architecture that schools invented in the nineteenth century grew to maturity as professional education. This educational model included subjects like Scripture, theology, ethics, and history, whose scholarly methods followed those of liberal arts disciplines, and pastoral care, religious education, church administration, and other subjects that were influenced by the scholarly methods of behavioral and social sciences. While specialized disciplines for the first group of subjects developed in the nineteenth century, relatively little disciplinary structure developed for the second group until the middle decades of the twentieth century. And as they developed into mature disciplines, ministry education could be understood fully as a form of professional education. The professional model was right for the times. It provided the education needed for ministers to assume their role among other professionals who functioned in an ever more complicated and sophisticated society. It fit the increasingly sophisticated demands of ministry, the increasingly bureaucratic structures of denominations, and the cultural status of the church.

Most of all, the professional model fit developments in higher education. Law, medicine, and theology had been long understood as professions, but "professionals" in these areas were being educated by a range of educational strategies as the nineteenth century came to an end. A Carnegie Foundation study of medical education in the early twentieth century made several negative assessments, and the responses in the ensuing decades revolutionized medical education. Medical schools became university based and, for the first time, began to require a college degree for admission. The new practices of accreditation of higher education were adapted to provide specialized quality assurance for medical schools in the first decades of the new century.[11] Legal education followed the lead of medical schools; another study by the Carnegie Foundation led to legal education being reorganized in a way similar to the way medical education had been. Law schools became housed in universities, for the most part, and a law-school-accrediting body was formed. Somewhat later, following a major study of ministry and theological education by Robert Kelly,[12] the Conference of Theological Schools voted to become an accrediting agency for Protestant theological schools in 1936, and the newly named American Association of Theological Schools promoted the idea of a college degree prior to entering seminary. At the beginning of the century, many theological schools were operating at what would best be termed associate or baccalaureate levels. The work of the accrediting agency over the next two decades contributed to the understanding of theological education as postbaccalaureate, professional education.

One of the greatest struggles of twentieth-century American Protestantism—the modernist-fundamentalist controversy—occurred in the 1920s. As in most theological battles, many factors precipitated this struggle, but a few stand out. Evolution and the biblical account of creation grabbed the headlines, but another factor was related to theological education. Most of the schools now identified with mainline Protestantism had adopted critical scholarly methods in the study of Scripture. These approaches had come kicking and screaming into the work of these schools in the late nineteenth century but had increasingly become an agreed-upon convention in the twentieth. The academic guilds that these schools helped form became influential forces in the definition of methods that characterized scholarly credibility. This critical study of the Bible, however, was perceived as a threat to orthodox faith, and this perception led to the founding of several seminaries and the formation of splinter and protest denominations, many of which became part of post–World War II evangelical Protestantism. If victory had been declared at the time the modernist-fundamentalist struggles waned, it would have been by the modernists. The Presbyterian and Congregationalist schools, the Methodist schools, many Lutheran and Reformed schools, and some of the Baptist schools in the North had made peace with modernity, even embraced it. The American Association of Theological Schools voted to begin accreditation in the 1930s, when the controversy was over. While the rhetoric and most of the reality of this action were related to educational issues and needs, it is not a coincidence that almost all the schools initially accredited were related to the religious bodies on the "modernist" side.

Growth and Complexity following World War II

The era after World War II could not have begun more auspiciously for mainline Protestants. Soldiers returned from war to work or to pursue an education funded by the GI Bill, to get married and have children, and, for an unusually large number, to go to church. Protestant congregations grew, Christian education buildings were erected, and, as suburbs began to grow, new congregations were started. Protestant seminaries shared in this fortuitous time. Enrollments increased, new buildings were erected, scholarship advanced, and the structures that had been built served this time well and provided resources for adapting to new demands. Mainline Protestants had become distinguishable from evangelical Protestants, and the mainline was dominant, the seeming heir of the legacy of the culture's informally established religion. The mainline Protestant mood may not have been triumphalist, but it was surely optimistic.

Then, for reasons much explored but still not fully understood, things began to change. Membership plateaued in the 1960s and began to decline. The dominance of the mainline made it possible to assume at first that the decline was an interruption, but the following decades undercut that assumption. Over the course of the final third of the century, denominational structures weakened and membership in many but not all congregations declined.

Initially mainline Protestant seminaries were able to resist the effects of this numerical decline. They found revenue sources in gifts from individual donors, increased tuition, and endowments that, even with market fluctuations, increased in value. Schools that had served only students from one denomination sustained their enrollment by welcoming students of many denominations. The fundamental shifts afoot in the denominations and congregations, as well as the social location of mainline Protestants in the culture, began to affect the seminaries.

Mainline Protestant seminaries maintained the freestanding structure they had invented, with the exception of the university-related divinity schools. What was a strength in the nineteenth and much of the twentieth century, however, has become a twofold threat in the twenty-first century. First, special-purpose higher education institutions have a narrow educational bandwidth. While they are ideally suited to educate religious leaders, the declining number of these potential leaders threatens their educational purpose and institutional stability. Second, degree-granting graduate schools in this century require significant financial resources, which constitutes a harsh reality for financially strapped schools. The result is that many freestanding seminaries are forced to consider merging with other seminaries or larger educational institutions.

As a group of schools, mainline Protestant seminaries are the oldest. Age grants benefits and bestows burdens. A primary institutional benefit is endowments. Although fewer in number than evangelical Protestant schools, mainline schools hold more than three times the endowment, and these endowments have helped fund them at a time when denominational strength has declined and revenue sources have become more strained. At the same time, facilities that may be architecturally significant but that no longer meet educational needs and require expensive repair and renovation can become a burden.

Mainline denominations began the twenty-first century with a very different future than the one with which they began the twentieth century. The privilege, financial capacity, and numeric strength that mainline Protestants enjoyed had dissipated. It is not clear why this happened, but the mighty mainline had been minimized, and that reality is a major influence on the seminaries related to these denominations. Many mainline seminaries have the financial and institutional resources, the balance of educational capacity and imagination, and the administrative ability not only to do well but also to provide leadership to the religious communities they serve. Others, especially schools that are distant from population centers, or that have overspent their endowments or never accrued one, or that have been ineffective in establishing a constituency of individual donors, will not do well in this century. At a time when a great deal of innovation is needed, many have little risk capital, and at a time when schools need maximum freedom to find their way to the future, they are operating with limited freedom. This century will likely result in many more institutional changes.

Concluding Reflections on Mainline Protestant Theological Education

Many mainline Protestant schools have histories that begin in colonial America. They are old enough to have undergone many changes. They changed from colleges to predominantly free-standing theological schools. They changed to accommodate the profound shifts that the modern era brought to the country. They changed their primary educational emphases from a general study of divinity to specialized professional education for ministry. These changes, and many more, reflect three influential forces that I have already mentioned: religion, culture, and higher education. These schools are in the midst of yet more change, and their future will be influenced by these three factors as much as their past has been.

Roman Catholic Theological Education

By 1790, national independence from England had been gained, a constitution for the United States had been ratified, George Washington had been elected the nation's first president, Harvard was almost 150 years old, and the College of William and Mary had reached the centennial of its founding. The Protestant presence was dominant. Roman Catholics numbered only thirty thousand, mostly in Pennsylvania and Maryland, and were served by thirty-five priests. Although its presence grew and changed, until Vatican II Catholicism tended to function apart from Protestant life and certainly apart from Protestant theological education. The culture, history, and educational practices of Roman Catholic schools differed from those of Protestant schools. If Protestants of the nineteenth and early twentieth centuries made up the quasi-established church, Catholics were the religious other and invented a religious and social culture separate from much of mainstream American life. For this discussion, I divide Roman Catholic theological education into three historical periods: (1) from the early years to the mid-nineteenth century, (2) from the mid-nineteenth century to World War II, and (3) after World War II.

Early Years

Jesuit missionaries arrived in what is now Maryland in 1662 and attended to the Roman Catholic population in the colonies for the next 150 years. For many reasons, mostly tied to power struggles among European monarchies and between them and the church, Pope Clement XIV suppressed the work of the Jesuits in 1773. The papal order was absolute, calling for the church to "suppress and abolish the said company . . . deprive it of all activity whatever." It left the Maryland Jesuits without status in the Roman Catholic Church, although they were allowed to continue to function as priests under the apostolic authority of a prelate in England. This ecclesiastical accountability to England did not sit well with Catholics in a country that had just won its independence, and the former Jesuits petitioned Rome to acknowledge the national status of the United States and to permit the formation of a diocese. The petition was granted, and in 1789 John Carroll was ordained a bishop of the single Catholic diocese in America.

Carroll wrote that "the object nearest to my heart is to establish a college on this continent for the education of youth, which might at the same time be a seminary for future clergymen."[13] His desire to found a seminary was problematic, however, because there were no Catholic theological scholars in the United States. The Jesuits, who had been in the colonies and had run more colleges and seminaries in other countries than any other single Roman Catholic entity, had been eliminated by papal decree. An intermediary approached Carroll and suggested that the Society of Saint Sulpice might be willing to operate a seminary in the new United States. The Society was founded in seventeenth-century France in the context of Catholic religious renewal and in response to the need for more educated and spiritually formed priests. Its members were diocesan priests, and its mission was to operate diocesan seminaries with "a methodology for spirituality, for community life, and for pedagogy."[14] However, in the late eighteenth century, the anticlericalism of the French Revolution threatened the Society's work. At its most violent, the anticlerical movement took the lives of several Sulpicians and closed its seminaries in France. Even though Carroll wanted an educational institution for Catholics, he did not think that the diocese could support a seminary. After discussions, the Society "agreed to pay for their own voyage, to maintain the seminary, and to supply the priests and three or four French seminarians who could adapt to the American language and customs."[15] Four priests and five seminarians arrived in Baltimore in 1791. Later that year, the first Catholic seminary on American soil was inaugurated, a school now known as St. Mary's Seminary and University. St. Mary's was also the first freestanding theological school in the nation. The suppression of the Jesuits, American independence from England, the French Revolution, and the authorization for a diocese by the Vatican had all contributed to the school's founding.

Roman Catholic seminaries, for the most part, were founded as freestanding institutions not related to Catholic colleges and universities,[16] in contrast to the earliest forms of Protestant theological education that were founded as colleges and universities.

They also differed in terms of ecclesiastical control. Diocesan Catholic seminaries operated under the direct control of the bishop, even when they were run by the Sulpicians. While Protestant schools were typically under the control of a denomination, the structures of the Protestant denominations did not allow for the intimate level of oversight that a diocesan bishop exercised. Perhaps most importantly, Catholic education of priests, heavily influenced by the Sulpicians and also the Society of St. Vincent, employed pedagogical strategies and goals that differed from nineteenth-century Protestant theological education. It was more focused on spirituality and socialization in a hierarchical church, while the Protestant version, with its roots in early colleges and universities, was more academic. The combination of a growing Catholic population, the capacity for theological education provided by the Sulpicians, and financial grants from some European mission societies contributed to the growth in number of Catholic diocesan seminaries.

The thirty thousand Catholics in America when St. Mary's was founded had grown to over one hundred thousand by 1810, and the single diocese for all of America had expanded into dioceses in New York, Philadelphia, Boston, Bardstown (Kentucky), and, with the Louisiana Purchase, New Orleans. By 1842, twenty-two seminaries enrolled 277 seminarians.

From Mid-Nineteenth Century to World War II

From the last half of the nineteenth century to the first decades of the twentieth century was a period of enormous immigration to the United States, and Catholic immigrants were among the most numerous.[17] Catholics in the United States grew from three million in 1860 to six million by 1882. In 1860, Catholics constituted 5 percent of the US population, and by 1906, 17 percent. While the early Catholic immigrants to Maryland (a colony to which they were initially welcomed but were later opposed, by Puritans) and Pennsylvania (a colony founded by Quakers, who did not establish a church) were primarily English or German, later immigrants came from Ireland and southern and eastern

Europe. These later groups of immigrants, especially, were often poor, with limited education, and greeted with suspicion by white Protestants. Toward the end of the nineteenth century, No Irish Need Apply signs could be seen in shops in New York and Boston. Racial classifications stratified whiteness in ways that separated southern and eastern European features and skin color from English and northern European features, and questions were even raised whether darker-skinned eastern and southern Europeans fit the 1790 statute that limited American naturalized citizenship to "free white persons." The anti-Catholic prejudice had both religious and racial roots, which together conspired to form the ugliest of human prejudices.

While Protestantism in the colonies reflected breaks with predecessor Protestant groups in England and Europe or honored newly formed religious sensitivities that matured in the United States, the Roman Catholic Church in the United States was not an American invention and was not formed in protest of Rome, and Catholics generally did not immigrate to escape religious persecution. The church in America was an ecclesial immigrant church that served an immigrant people, and in many ways provided a powerful force for unity among diverse immigrant groups.

For the most part, Catholic immigrants were concentrated in ethnic neighborhoods in urban areas. These neighborhoods provided a shared language and social structure as people adjusted to life in America. Most Catholic neighborhoods had a parish church, and, by the end of the nineteenth century, many of these parishes had established primary schools because anti-Catholic prejudice and Protestant domination of the public schools left Catholic parents and clergy fearful that Catholic children would be turned into crypto-Protestants.

The combination of anti-Catholic prejudice that isolated Catholics from mainstream American culture, ethnic neighborhoods, and parish churches and schools provided resources that shaped a Catholic subculture until World War II. The organizing center of that culture was the church, and the Catholic Church seems to have held Catholics together in ways that Protestantism did not do for Protestants.

During this period, several characteristics of Catholic education for priesthood became evident. The first was the increased number of schools. Some were founded by dioceses as the number of dioceses grew, and others were founded to serve particular ethnic communities. Catholic religious institutes established seminaries, sometimes for the training of their own members and sometimes for the training of diocesan priests. Four Benedictine monastic communities that sponsored seminaries were founded between 1846 and 1882. After the suppression of the Jesuits was reversed, a Jesuit seminary was established in New York, followed by several others. The Dominicans founded three schools; the Franciscans established two, as did the Oblates of Mary Immaculate. The result was a diverse system of seminaries that reflected the diverse structures of the Roman Catholic Church.

A second characteristic was the unique educational direction and goals of these schools. Bishop Spalding argued in an 1881 speech that "if it were possible that we should be compelled to choose between a virtuous but ignorant priesthood and a priesthood which had high mental cultivation but would lack righteousness and the spiritual mind, the choice ought not to be difficult." He went on to say that both are needed and quoted Augustine, who (building on Aristotle) wrote that "without knowledge it is not possible to have the virtues which make life holy." While he advocated for an institution that would advance Catholic intellectual life, he argued that "the ecclesiastical seminary is not a school of intellectual culture, either here in America or elsewhere and to imagine that it can become the instrument of intellectual culture is to cherish a delusion." A seminary, he continued, "must impart a certain amount of professional knowledge, fit its students to become more or less expert catechists, rubricists, and casuists, and its aim is to do this, and whatever mental improvement, if any, thence results, is accidental."[18] Spalding seemed to argue for priests who know how to do their job well and do it with spiritual sensitivity and holiness, but that the intellectual efforts that the church should mount would require other kinds of institutions.

A third characteristic relates to the structure and duration of study. The system adopted by the bishops in the 1880s consisted of minor and major seminaries. The minor seminary was a six-year program for boys and adolescents. Education began early because of a perception that youth, "unless rightly trained[,] is inclined to follow the pleasures of the world." The United States had no child labor laws or compulsory high school education at this point, older boys and early teenagers often began work in the fields or factories, and the church hoped to make a claim on them before they were otherwise occupied. This program focused on general studies, language proficiency in English and Latin, and doctrine. The major seminary was a six-year program of study that followed education in the minor seminary. The first two years of study focused on philosophy, especially Thomistic philosophy as it was understood after 1870, and the other four on theology, which consisted of "dogmatic-scholastic theology, moral theology, biblical exegesis, church history, canon law, theoretical and practical aspects of liturgy, and sacred eloquence."[19] Over time, the major seminaries "developed a pedagogy with instruction based on manuals . . . digests of formal doctrinal treatises with opposing positions refuted and the Catholic teaching defended."[20] These manuals, with their polemical and apologetic approach, "were used widely in seminary formation in France, the United States and elsewhere . . . [and] were the primary compendia of Catholic truth at the time for priestly formation."[21] This system with minor and major seminaries continued as the dominant pattern for priestly education until Vatican II.

Finally, as Bishop Spalding had argued, Catholic seminaries did not come to serve as a center of Catholic intellectual life. The Catholic colleges and universities undertook that task. Georgetown University, which granted its first baccalaureate degrees in 1817; the University of Notre Dame, founded in 1844; and Boston College, founded in 1863, all had relatively humble beginnings but are currently ranked in the top 10 percent of US national universities. All of them, and many more, contribute to a Catholic intellectual mission.

These decades ended with a huge Catholic population; a lively Catholic culture that involved community; ethnic celebrations; parish and Catholic schools; ample candidates for priesthood and communities of women religious; Catholic hospitals, orphanages, and homes for the aged; seminaries with large facilities and enrollments; and a large number of Catholic colleges and universities. The immigrants had arrived and made a home; the immigrant church had flourished.

World War II and Following

World War II marked a major change in American Catholicism. During the war, Catholics fought alongside Protestants, and both fought along with Jews, who before World War II had often lived (or been legally forced to live) in separate neighborhoods. Perhaps for the first time, American Protestants, Catholics, and Jews were engaged in a common struggle that brought them all together under the most intense of circumstances. The makings of an America of "Protestant, Catholic, and Jew" had begun. After the war, the Servicemen's Readjustment Act (popularly known as the GI Bill) made it possible for millions of returning servicemen, including Roman Catholics, to pursue higher education. In the 1950s, suburbs emerged and attracted many adults who had grown up in ethnic urban neighborhoods. The Catholics who moved to the suburbs were still Catholic and, like most Americans of the 1950s, religiously observant, but their children did not grow up in the Catholic culture that had existed in neighborhoods comprising a parish church, a parish school, and ethnic celebrations.

As American Catholic culture was dissipating, the church was embarking on its most definitive twentieth-century event: Vatican II. The reforms issued out of the Council moved the American church into a world it had not known before. Sister Katarina Schuth, OFM, the premier researcher on US Catholic theological education, has talked with me about how Vatican II had changed virtually everything in the religious life to which she was called. The academic career she pursued, the seminary where she taught, and the pattern of theological education that she studied were all changed in profound ways because of the reforms Vatican II set in motion.

Optatam Totius (OT)[22] served as the Council's primary decree regarding priestly education. It granted bishops authority to develop seminary programs that fit local needs and conventions. Along with affirming the importance of philosophy and theology, *OT* brought a fresh emphasis on Scripture in priestly formation, maintaining that "students are to be formed with particular care in the study of the Bible, which ought to be, as it were, the soul of theology."

The permission to regionalize patterns of theological education and the mandate that national councils of bishops establish basic norms for seminaries resulted in reforms in the seminaries in the United States. The system of minor and major seminaries was changed to a system of college seminaries and postbaccalaureate institutions called theologates.[23] College seminaries were designed to conduct a range of general undergraduate studies along with significant concentration on philosophy in the context of spiritual formation and discernment on whether graduates should pursue further theological study. Other college level programs functioned as residential houses of formation for college seminarians who attended a Catholic college or university to earn a baccalaureate degree. The college seminaries assumed some of the advanced work that had been done in minor seminaries and some of the elementary work, especially philosophy, done in the major seminaries. The seminaries, or theologates, became postbaccalaureate institutions that focused on theological, biblical, and pastoral training in the context of a sustained program of spiritual formation.

Prior to Vatican II, the minor and major seminaries had granted ecclesiastical degrees. After the Council, college seminaries granted baccalaureate degrees and the seminaries granted master's degrees, thus providing a currency in American higher education that was not previously available. These "civil" degrees created the need for accreditation, the traditional pattern of quality assurance in higher education. The college seminaries sought accreditation by regional accrediting agencies, and by 1968, fifteen seminaries had begun the accreditation process with what is now the Association of Theological Schools in the United States and Canada. By 1984, forty-nine Catholic seminaries were either accredited or preaccredited members of ATS. The Catholic seminaries aligned their educational patterns and practices with Protestants even as they carefully maintained accountability to ecclesiastical norms and expectations.

While the seminaries were changing, so were the numbers of priests and vowed women religious. In 1965, almost 60,000 diocesan and religious priests and almost 180,000 religious sisters served a parish-connected Catholic population of 46.3 million.[24] In 2017, 37,181 priests and 45,605 religious sisters served 68.5 million parish-connected Catholics. While the number of parish-connected Catholics has *increased* 50 percent across these decades, the number of priests has *declined* almost 40 percent, and the number of religious sisters, almost 80 percent. It is an amazing and unparalleled phenomenon in the composition of leadership in any religious entity in the United States. In 1965, 549 Catholic parishes were without a resident priest/pastor. The number of parishes without resident priests in 2017 was over 3,500. Seminaries also saw a marked decline in enrollment. In 1965, there were 8,325 graduate-level seminary students, and in 2017, there were 3,405, a 60 percent decline. The result has been mergers and closures and a further realignment of seminaries. The changes have been massive and dramatic, but churchly structures, for the most part, have been able to absorb them, and the current number of seminaries is adequate for the enrollment of what has become a stable number of seminarians.[25]

The seminaries have also addressed a pattern of leadership that has emerged since Vatican II. In 1995, 10,674 lay professional ministers worked in Catholic parishes. They led religious education programs and music ministries, provided ministries of pastoral care and social witness, and in other ways supported the ministry of Catholic parishes—but they were not priests, brothers, or religious sisters. Twenty years later, in 2015, their number was almost 18,000. Many of these lay professional ministers have sought theological education, and the enrollment of laypersons in Roman Catholic seminaries now equals the number of men studying for priesthood. In addition to the changes brought about by *OT*, another exhortation, *Pastores dabo vobis* (*PV*), issued by Pope John Paul II in 1992, brought even more change. It refined the pattern of priestly education to focus on pastoral, intellectual, personal, and spiritual formation. These elements had been nascent since *OT* was adopted, but *PV* made them the foundation of contemporary Roman Catholic priestly education.

The US Conference of Catholic Bishops adopted the *Program of Priestly Formation* (*PPF*), now in its fifth edition, which identifies the ecclesiastical norms to which seminaries are accountable. It sets the formation of persons for priesthood on four interrelated and interconnected elements, or "pillars": spiritual, pastoral, human, and intellectual.

Intellectual formation involves education in theology, church history, and biblical studies that, according to *OT*, should be taught "so that students will correctly draw out Catholic doctrine from divine revelation, profoundly penetrate it, and make it the food of their own spiritual lives."

Pastoral formation involves the development of the homiletical, liturgical, leadership, and educational capacities to lead parishes in worship, witness, and education. After Vatican II, Roman Catholic formation for priesthood also required that seminarians be involved in parish or other ministerial work, something earlier patterns of formation had not so extensively required. These two pillars look very much like theological education in Protestant schools.

The other two pillars are more unique to Catholic seminary education. The *PPF* describes the goal of spiritual formation as "to live in intimate and unceasing union with God the Father through his Son, Jesus Christ, in the Holy Spirit" and to achieve "a spirituality of communion rooted in the mystery of the Triune God and lived out in practical ways in the mystery of ecclesial communion."[26] The goal of human formation is to cultivate the "human personality of the priest to be a bridge and not an obstacle for others in their meeting with Jesus Christ the redeemer of the human race."[27] Human formation has many dimensions, including moral character, personal maturity, relational capacity, and faithful stewardship of material possessions. To implement these norms, Catholic seminarians work with "formators" for human and spiritual direction. The human formator guides a seminarian and helps him process strengths and weaknesses in his emotions and relationships. He does much of what a therapist might do, with a goal of mature and responsible personhood. The spiritual director is a different person, whose task is to accompany and guide the student in the development of his spirituality. These tasks of giving substantive and sustained attention to personal and spiritual issues, funded by the seminary, for all four years of study for the ministerial priesthood, make this kind of theological education formational in a way not characteristic in Protestant theological education.

If Roman Catholic theological education gives sustained attention to human formation and spiritual growth, then the incidence of criminal sexual abuse of minors by Roman Catholic clergy that has dominated the religious news much of this century could indicate that something must be terribly wrong with this model. The cause of this criminal abuse is much debated—suspects include the internal fraternity of an all-male priesthood, the authority structures in the church, and the requirement of celibacy—but of greatest interest in the current discussion is its educational implications. The current pattern of formational theological education is an invention of the early 1990s, and theological education for priests after the early 1990s was radically different from the education of priests before then. Could this educational change be related to sexual abuse of minors?

A study of clerical sexual abuse of minors between 1950 and 2002 commissioned by the US Conference of Catholic Bishops and conducted by the John Jay College of Criminal Justice found that the "majority of priests with allegations of abuse were ordained between 1950 and 1979 (68%). Priests ordained prior to 1950 accounted for 21.3% of the allegations, and priests ordained after 1979 accounted for 10.7% of allegations."[28] An investigation in Pennsylvania, first reported in 2018, identified more than three hundred priests with allegations of sexual misconduct of minors found in the records of six dioceses. This report has many problems, as Peter Steinfels has demonstrated,[29] but I sampled almost half of the individual profiles of accused priests, and in this sample 60 percent had completed seminary in the 1960s or earlier, and 40 percent in the 1970s or later. Of this later group, 2 percent completed seminary in the 1990s and the first decade of the new century. While more than one interpretation is possible, the agreement between the John Jay study (priests ordained after 1979 accounted for 10.7 percent of cases reported) and the Pennsylvania report (just over 9 percent of all reported offenses were by priests ordained after 1980) suggests that something has reduced the number of offenses since the early 1990s. No doubt the decrease is due to several factors, including changes in episcopal oversight and reporting, screening of potential candidates, changes in the ways offenders have been dealt with by the church, and aggressive public scrutiny. It is possible, however, that the significant changes in the way candidates for the ministerial priesthood have been educated since the early 1990s, especially with its focus on human formation, have played a role in decreasing the number of incidents of clerical abuse.

Concluding Thoughts about Roman Catholic Theological Education

The immigrant church that was kept to the sidelines of nine-teenth- and early twentieth-century American life has become the most dominant Christian presence in the twenty-first century. And, while the forms and patterns of Catholic theological education varied significantly from Protestant forms, the influences contributing to its development, in my opinion, were similar: culture, church and religious practices, and practices of higher education. As immigrants, Catholics were isolated from much of mainstream American culture and thus developed a rich and unifying culture of their own. That culture contributed to the shaping of theological education. Roman Catholic theological education has been and continues to be much more intricately connected to the church than is Protestant theological education. The changes in the church, such as Vatican II, have had a profound effect on the character of education and the strategies for education for the ministerial priesthood. Since Vatican II, Roman Catholic theological education has been bent in the direction of American higher education practices. In these ways Catholic theological education shows the influences of culture, church, and higher education.

Evangelical Theological Education

Evangelical theological education as it currently exists is, with a few exceptions, a twentieth-century invention, although many of the core characteristics of evangelical Protestantism are much older. These characteristics—such as a high view of the authority of Scripture, an emphasis on evangelism and personal conversion, and the importance of missions—were part of many strands of nineteenth-century Protestantism. There were more conservative and liberal versions, but the characteristics were ubiquitous among Baptists and Presbyterians, as well as Methodists and Congregationalists, and reflected the influence of the awakenings that had shaped much of nineteenth-century Protestantism. Fault lines, however, began to develop in the late nineteenth century that continued through the first half of the twentieth century, and as those fault lines widened, evangelical theological schools were founded. They were also founded as an outgrowth of new religious movements and immigration patterns. While a few of these schools harken back to the late nineteenth and early twentieth century, the overwhelming majority have been founded since World War II. In 2018, of the approximately 280 ATS member institutions in the United States and Canada, 124 were classified as evangelical Protestant. These evangelically identified schools together enroll about 65 percent of all the students in ATS member schools. Understanding these schools is enhanced by attention to the different cultural and religious moments from which they emerged and the institutional and educational patterns that characterize their work.

Historical Moments and Founding Origins

Some historians argue that the separation of Protestantism into its mainline and evangelical branches began with the American struggle over slavery and the Civil War. Methodists, Presbyterians, and Baptists split national denominations into northern and southern structures in the years prior to the war. The southern branches affirmed slavery, either directly or indirectly, and generally came to hold conservative theological perspectives. The northern branches reflected different views about slavery, and over time adopted more progressive theological views. The Protestant evangelical consensus that characterized the first half of the nineteenth century began to dissipate. Southern Baptist Theological Seminary was founded in the nineteenth century in the context of this separation and its aftermath, and currently identifies with evangelical Protestantism, although this identification was contested before the conservative resurgence in the Southern Baptist Convention in the 1980s and '90s.[30]

The late nineteenth through early twentieth century was a time of considerable cultural change in America. Fundamental social structures were changing as the United States population became increasingly urban; as the Industrial Revolution contributed to new economic structures; as scientific advances generated new knowledge and, in the process, contested some religious positions (like evolution versus creation); and as higher education changed with the development of public institutions and the research university. Sociologist James Davison Hunter, in an early analysis of evangelical Protestantism, argued that "no religion transcends social structures." Hunter noted that the accumulation of these cultural changes contributed to a "Protestantism divided into conservative and liberal communities of faith" in which "each faction represented and continues to represent distinct responses to these broader changes . . . one, an aggressive capitulation to the world of modernity; the other, a combination of reluctant accommodation and defensive reaction to it."[31]

New scholarly approaches brought significant questions to old assumptions about the Bible and its teaching, from who authored the books to how they should be interpreted. These struggles affected much of Protestant theological education, as I noted earlier. Southern Baptist Theological Seminary, Union Theological Seminary in New York, and Princeton Theological Seminary all had major controversies over faculty who were using new scholarly methods to teach the Bible. What differed was how each resolved it: Southern dismissed a faculty member who used modern scholarly methods in the 1870s; Union severed its Presbyterian connections rather than dismiss an accused professor in the 1890s; and some conservative faculty members at Princeton, having lost control of the faculty, left to start a new seminary in the 1920s.

These controversies, along with the modernist-fundamentalist struggles in the 1920s, resulted in the immediate formation of several seminaries. Westminster Seminary was founded by the faculty members who left Princeton; Northern Baptist Theological Seminary was founded in Chicago as a protest to perceived theological liberalism in the Northern Baptist Convention (and the University of Chicago Divinity School), as was Eastern Baptist Theological Seminary in Philadelphia (now Palmer Seminary of Eastern University). The struggle contributed to the establishment of other schools founded after World War II. Western Seminary (Oregon) and Denver Seminary, for example, were started by Baptists who exited the Northern Baptist Convention in the late 1940s. Fuller Theological Seminary was founded in 1947 by a popular radio evangelist, and like many of the schools founded from these roots, moved beyond fundamentalism early in its history.[32] Many schools founded after World War II have held to a conservative theology while abandoning the hard-edged fundamentalist posturing of the early part of the twentieth century. As biblical scholarship in these schools developed, many of their faculty adopted the critical methods for the study of Scripture that were the cause of uproar decades earlier, although some have used those methods in service of more theologically conservative conclusions.

Some nineteenth-century immigrant groups contributed to founding several schools that would now be considered evangelical Protestant. Covenanters and Baptists, for example, emigrated from Scandinavia and founded the predecessor institutions of North Park Theological Seminary, Bethel Theological Seminary, and Trinity Evangelical Divinity School.

The growth of urban centers in the late nineteenth and early twentieth century, fueled in part by immigration, led to the founding of a new kind of theological school. A. B. Simpson, who founded the Christian and Missionary Alliance, described such schools as "institutions less technical and elaborate than [the] ordinary theological seminary, and designed to afford the same specific preparation for direct missionary work, and to meet the wants of that large class, both men and women, who do not wish a formal ministerial preparation, but an immediate equipment for usefulness as lay workers."[33] Dwight L. Moody raised money for the Chicago Evangelization Society by explaining, "I believe we have got to have gap-men—men who are trained to do city mission work. Every city mission in this country and Europe has been a failure . . . because the men are not trained."[34] Bible colleges were a new pattern of theological education to get Christian workers to the urban mission field as soon as possible with the practical, how-to knowledge needed to do that work. At a time when all theological education was denominationally affiliated, these schools tended to be non- and sometimes antidenominational. They saw themselves as alternatives to rather than competitors of theological schools, and they focused extensively on practical training. With their emphasis on laypersons, they became some of the first theological institutions to educate women for ministerial work in city and foreign missions. In the United States, the Bible colleges founded in Boston, New York, Chicago, and Los Angeles were the predecessor institutions of several contemporary evangelical theological schools: Gordon-Conwell Theological Seminary near Boston; Nyack Theological Seminary near New York City; Moody Bible Institute in Chicago; and Talbot School of Theology of Biola University in Los Angeles.

Perhaps the most powerful religious movement of the twentieth century began in April 1906, when a revival broke out among domestic and custodial workers in Los Angeles. It signaled the beginning of the Pentecostal movement. This movement, which by the end of the twentieth century had influenced other forms of Protestantism in worship patterns if not theology, spawned several US denominations, including the Assemblies of God; Church of God, Cleveland; Church of God in Christ; and the United Pentecostal Church. By the end of the twentieth century, this movement, despite some anti-intellectual inclinations among its earliest adherents, had founded Bible colleges, Christian liberal arts colleges, and theological schools, including the Oral Roberts University Graduate School of Theology and Ministry (first accredited by the ATS in 1980), Pentecostal Theological Seminary (1989),[35] Assemblies of God Theological Seminary (1992), Regent University School of Divinity (1993), and Urshan Graduate School of Theology (2010). The Charles Mason Seminary was founded as part of the Interdenominational Theological Center (ITC) in 1970 and shared in ITC's accreditation from its founding.

Also in the early twentieth century, a form of Wesleyan theology emerged that emphasized personal holiness, sanctification, and missions. Holiness is crucial to all Wesleyan theology, but more conservative groups began to separate from the main Methodist bodies in the late nineteenth century because they perceived that the importance of holiness had been devalued.

Conservative Methodists, from both within and without the main Methodist denominations, founded Asbury Theological Seminary (1938). Denominations with a focus on holiness then formed, among them the Church of God, Anderson, which eventually established the Anderson University School of Theology in Indiana (1965), and the Church of the Nazarene, which founded Nazarene Theological Seminary (1970) in Kansas City.

Other religious winds also contributed to the rise of evangelical theological schools in the twentieth century. The Bible conferences of the early part of the century, with an emphasis on commonsense understanding of Scripture and a particular interpretation of biblical prophecy, cultivated a nondenominational community of congregations and followers of conference speakers like C. I. Scofield. Dallas Theological Seminary grew out of the Bible conferences, including the dispensationalism popularized by Scofield's teaching in the Bible conferences and the notes of the Scofield Reference Bible.[36]

In the late twentieth century, another cycle of immigration to the United States contributed to evangelical theological education. These immigrants were from Taiwan, China, and Korea, and, while distinctive, they registered in the United States as "evangelical" in theology—perhaps reflecting the Christianity endowed to them by nineteenth- and early twentieth-century US missionaries. By the turn of the twenty-first century, Asians and Asian Americans constituted the largest group of racial/ethnic students in evangelical theological schools. While most of this enrollment was in historically white schools, Asians founded new schools to serve Asian communities. Logos Evangelical Seminary, of the Taiwanese Evangelical Church, was the first seminary accredited by the Commission on Accrediting of the ATS, with Mandarin as its primary language of instruction (1999).[37] The ATS now has eleven member schools whose primary language of instruction is Korean, Cantonese, or Mandarin.

Evangelical theological schools at the end of the second decade of this century are an interesting amalgamation of institutions. A few have been in existence since the days of the nineteenth-century evangelical consensus, and others have been founded in part to continue tenets of that consensus perceived to have been abandoned or lost. They constitute several broad Christian families: Baptist, Presbyterian/Reformed, Wesleyan, Pentecostal, and nondenominational. They reflect communities that construct religious practices in different forms. Some privilege experiential religious practices, others privilege rationalist practices, and still others privilege quietist and interior religious practices. Both the schools and transdenominational American evangelicals find their binding affinity in their shared commitments to a high view of Scripture, missions and evangelism, the importance of personal faith (often including conversion), and a generally conservative theology.

The twentieth century began with the marginalization of conservative Protestant commitments and their apparent defeat in the fundamentalist battles of the 1920s. The century ended with evangelicals being the dominant Protestant presence in America. Evangelical schools have become equally dominant. By the end of the twentieth century, more evangelical schools had been founded since World War II than the total number of mainline Protestant schools that survived from the nineteenth into the twentieth century.

As I write in 2020, evangelical Protestants are most often identified with the patterns of worship they have invented, their close connection with conservative Republican politics, and the megachurches they have founded in the past fifty years. It would be a mistake, however, to assume that these characteristics dominate evangelical theological education. Evangelical schools serve evangelical Protestants, but the schools are typically not intellectual apologists for popularized perspectives of evangelicals. Many evangelical schools, like one studied ethnographically in the 1990s,[38] understand part of their mission to be reforming popular evangelicalism. If the schools are not best characterized by the broader evangelical Protestant community, then what does characterize them and how do they differ from mainline Protestant schools?

Institutional and Educational Characteristics

Because evangelical theological schools are almost exclusively twentieth-century institutions, they bear many of the institutional and educational characteristics common to all Protestant schools. The requirements for degrees, the array of faculty positions, and the character of administrative offices do not distinguish evangelical and mainline theological schools, with a few notable exceptions.

Two primary reasons account for this similarity. The first is the ontology of a graduate theological school, whatever its denominational or theological commitments. They are *schools*: they have students to recruit and educate; faculty to appoint, support, and in some cases manage; administrators to attend to a variety of strategic and detailed efforts; boards to guide and govern; budgets to raise and manage; facilities to acquire and maintain; and academic standards to establish and sustain. The commonality of these tasks in graduate theological education nurtures a certain homogeneity in the institutional character of theological schools. The second reason is that the evangelical schools are members of the ATS and accredited by its Commission on Accrediting, which provides a homogenizing influence on the institutional forms while permitting theological diversity.

These schools also distinguish themselves in several ways. Many evangelical schools were founded as nondenominational seminaries, such as Dallas, Fuller, and Gordon-Conwell. By contrast, virtually all mainline schools were founded with strong denominational ties. These nondenominational schools comprise a genuinely new invention in theological education. They were founded by the vision and efforts of an individual or group, apart from accountability to an ecclesial body. They have been funded by student tuition and gifts from individual donors rather than grants from denominations. They have cultivated a constituency of congregations or parachurch agencies to identify ministry positions for graduates; and to attract students who came from denominations and may return to them after seminary, most have needed to advocate their value to (often suspicious) denominations. These characteristics have proven to be advantageous.

Over the past few decades, theological schools have needed to devote increasing attention to their institutional mission. Many denominational seminaries had operated as a unit of a church body, and their missions were sufficiently tied to their denominations that schools did not have to attend closely to their institutional mission. As denominations have weakened, schools have needed to give more careful attention to their institutional missions—to the vocation to which they perceived themselves to be called. Accrediting standards required all schools to focus on mission, but for some schools, serious attention to mission was a new task. Twentieth-century nondenominational schools had been doing this all along.

The funding sources for many Protestant schools have changed over the past half century. Grants from denominations have declined as a percentage of total revenue, even if actual dollar amounts have not.[39] As a result, schools need to find funding elsewhere, primarily from individual donors and student tuition. Dependence on tuition revenue requires raising money from donors to support student scholarships and stipends, as well as negotiating the complex world of federally guaranteed student loans. Once again, the twentieth-century nondenominational schools had something of a head start in this. They had never had denominational money but had always depended on individual donors and tuition as primary revenue streams. Many nineteenth-century schools had the ballast of endowments that had accrued over time, and those invested resources cushioned the decline of denominational support, but the newer, twentieth-century schools did not have that cushion. They were forced to develop individual donors or go out of business.

The dependence on student tuition, greater for evangelical than mainline schools, contributed to the evangelical schools' more venturesome innovation in educational delivery and degree program offerings. The evangelical schools were among the first to offer extension site education, to develop multiple-campus models, and to develop distance-education programs. All these efforts were to meet missional objectives, of course, but they also provided access to a greater number of tuition-paying students.

The evangelical schools reflect academic attention to theological virtues that have characterized evangelical Protestants in noticeable ways: biblical studies, missions, and evangelism. These schools do not require more courses in Bible than do other seminaries, but they have continued the study of biblical languages that has been reduced in many other schools. The evangelical emphasis on missions is evident in these schools as well. In a review of ATS member schools that offered degrees with "missions" or some variant of that term in the title, 86 percent were classified as evangelical Protestant.[40] Evidence reflecting the evangelical commitment to evangelism also exists. In the data that schools reported to the ATS Commission on Accrediting in 2017, 66 percent of all faculty who had "evangelism" in their professorial titles were teaching in evangelical schools.

Evangelical schools have sought to advance intellectual effort in constituencies that had significant suspicions about intellectual effort in service to faith. This suspicion, if not an outright anti-intellectual spirit, was evident from the beginning. Historian Timothy George quotes J. J. Packer from the 1895 minutes of the Illinois Baptist General Association, who described typical seminary grads as "these pulpit dudes with kidded hands and velveted mouths preaching that 'unless you repent to some extent and be converted in a measure you will be damned in all probability.'"[41] Mark Noll has written: "To put it simply, the evangelical ethos is activistic, pragmatic, and utilitarian. It allows little space for broader or deeper intellectual effort because it is dominated by the urgencies of the moment."[42] Noll presses hard: "Fundamentalism, dispensational premillennialism, the Higher Life movement, and Pentecostalism were all evangelical strategies of survival in response to the religious crises of the late nineteenth century. In different ways, each preserved something essential to the Christian faith. But together they were a disaster for the life of the mind."[43]

Unlike Roman Catholic and most mainline Protestant theological schools, evangelical schools have contended with an underlying suspicion about intellectual effort, the most fundamental tool for their work. The result has been varied. Some scholars have avoided publishing, reframing the higher education maxim "publish *or* perish" as "publish *and* perish." Other scholars have focused on philological studies—important for biblical studies but not likely to attract much attention. Still others have engaged in modern forms of scholasticism. Many, however, have addressed issues in ways that have advanced scholarship in important areas, and they have done so with the support of their institutions. Almost all evangelical schools adopt statements of faith to which faculty must subscribe, and guarantee freedom of inquiry within those bounds—a practice that is also true for Roman Catholic seminaries, although managed in a very different way. Of all the agencies and structures that serve evangelical Protestantism, theological schools are most deeply influenced by the intellectual suspicions that emerged early and have persisted long.

Like all Protestant schools, they are encountering increasingly difficult financial futures. Because they are generally newer institutions, they have not accrued the endowments that characterize some older schools and are more dependent on tuition for revenue, which makes them sensitive to changes in enrollment. After a half century of continuing growth, enrollment in evangelical schools leveled off and then declined slightly. Many schools discovered that their de facto business model was a growing enrollment with its corresponding growth in revenue—a business model that will not sustain a school with declining or even stable enrollment. An increase in the number of new schools over a fifty-year period combined with the initial decline in evangelical Protestants and the saturation of the evangelical student market will require these schools to change the way they address financial needs. According to annual reports submitted to ATS, 40 percent of freestanding evangelical schools reported expenses greater than adjusted revenue in 2017–2018, and the situation has not improved in the ensuing years.

Concluding Thoughts on Evangelical Protestant Theological Education

Evangelical theological education is affected by the same three overriding influences that marked mainline and Roman Catholic theological education: religion, higher education, and culture. It has been influenced by religious practices—from theological protests to new religious movements that have formed evangelical Protestantism. As a twentieth-century movement, its schools show the influence of prevailing higher education practices they embodied as they developed. And, even in startling ways, they show cultural influences. Evangelicals invented the modern Protestant megachurch at the same time that big box stores reformed American merchandizing and the cinema multiplex changed moviegoing. Evangelical schools adopted digital technology for instruction at the time digital innovations were changing the way corporations and government did business. In many ways, the evangelical movement has been the most culturally attuned religious presence of the last half of the twentieth century.

While the number of evangelical Protestants consistently increased during the last decades of the twentieth century, studies in the first decades of the current century indicate a different trend. Robert Putnam and David Campbell observed a decline in the percentage of the US population that identifies as evangelical Protestant and argued that "the evangelical boom that began in the 1970s was over by the early 1990s, nearly two decades ago. In twenty-first-century America, expansive evangelicalism is a feature of the past, not the present."[44] Robert Jones, using the same data source as Putnam and Campbell but limiting his analysis to whites, noted that white evangelicals had declined as a percentage of the population from 22 percent in 1998 to 18 percent in 2014.[45] The decline in the percentage of Americans who identify as evangelical Protestant has not been accompanied by a decline of attention to this group—particularly the close connection between white evangelicals and conservative American politics, religious authority, and their desire to shape American culture in an evangelical direction.[46] Evangelical Protestantism, however, is changing in this century. The cultural power it exercised in the first decades of the century will likely decline as the century matures, and the theological schools that were founded during its ascendancy will have to adjust to compensate for the decline.

Historically Black Theological Schools and Racial/Ethnic Students

James Cone has rightly described racism as America's original sin. And it is no exaggeration to think of American religion as its enabler. That original sin can extend even to the ways we try to think and talk about religion in America. A history of theological institutions organized by large ecclesial families is inherently problematic, primarily because it fails to do justice to the vitality of historically black theological schools. These schools have formed identities between and beyond categories organized with whiteness as a presumed norm; these categories also obscure the experiences of African American students and faculty within majority white theological schools. Hoping to interrupt the hold of whiteness on what we can see, I want to pay special attention to historically black theological schools and to the experiences of African Americans and other minoritized groups in theological education.

Historically Black Schools

The story of these schools can begin at many times and places, but I choose two. The first is just after the Civil War. Enslaved people had been freed without money or land. Most had been denied formal education. They did have religion. With some financial help from a Baptist in the North, a facility in Richmond, Virginia, was purchased for a school to educate black ministers.

The building had been used to house newly arrived Africans and "break" them in preparation for their sale as slaves. But it was transformed into a school now known as the Samuel DeWitt Proctor School of Theology of Virginia Union University. The school has provided education for African Americans for more than a century; its current enrollment is among the largest of historically black schools. It is hard to imagine a deeper or more dramatic transformation of a building's purpose.

The second story begins in Philadelphia shortly after the Revolutionary War. Methodists had gathered for worship one day at St. George's Methodist Church, and when blacks, including Richard Allen, went to the altar to pray, whites pulled them away. Allen, himself formerly enslaved in Delaware, subsequently led the formation of Bethel Methodist Church, served as its pastor, and worked to legally protect it from control by whites. Allen and Bethel led in the formation of the African Methodist Episcopal Church. The AME Church founded Payne Theological Seminary of Wilberforce University in 1891 in Wilberforce, Ohio, a community with a distinguished history as a stop on the Underground Railroad.

African American theological schools are all Protestant, but they do not fit easily into the mainline-evangelical dichotomy. Their story is one of blacks removed from the altar, relegated to the balcony, kept a safe distance from white religious spaces, and freed from slavery to become slaves of Jim Crow laws. It is the story of slaves who helped build Virginia Theological Seminary but could not attend, and whose labor earned fortunes that helped fund schools like the Southern Baptist Theological Seminary, which did not admit African Americans until after World War II. It is a story of underfunded theological schools that educationally outperform their material resources. Six historically black theological schools are ATS members, and one of them, the Interdenominational Theological Center, is a consortium of six schools that had been freestanding seminaries or related to historically black colleges or universities.

Racial/Ethnic Presence

But this story is also about the presence of students from minoritized racial and ethnic groups in theological schools. The number of these students has been increasing steadily, from less than 10 percent of total enrollment in the early 1970s to 35 percent at present. African Americans constitute about 12 percent of enrollment in ATS schools, which is proportionate to their percentage in the American population. Persons of Asian descent compose about 9 percent of theological school students and 4 percent of the population. Hispanics constitute about 5 percent of ATS enrollment and about 14 percent of the US population. The overall enrollment of theological schools declined almost 10 percent over the last decade, and while enrollment has now leveled off, its current strength is attributable solely to the increasing presence of students of color.

The intersections of race and the three ecclesial families by which this history is organized occur in different places. Each family has a different story, with a different dominant racial/ethnic group, and theological constructions that address issues of racism differently.[47] None of them has a theology that makes racism sinless, and none is free of the legacy or contemporary practice of that sin.

Since World War II, Catholic immigrants have been Asian, primarily from Southeast Asia, and Hispanic/Latino/a immigrants have been primarily from Mexico, Central America, and South America. If present trends hold, the US Catholic Church will be majority Hispanic by the end of the 2020s—the first historically white church body in the United States to develop a majority comprised of a different race or ethnicity. The largest percentage of persons from historically minoritized racial/ethnic groups in evangelical Protestant schools is Asian. Almost 70 percent of all students of Asian descent enrolled in ATS schools are in evangelical Protestant schools, including the recently founded Asian-language schools. While evangelical schools have a large enrollment of Asians and a sizable enrollment of Hispanics, they have a relatively low enrollment of African Americans. Even though their conservative theology fits that of the historically black churches, the alignment of their constituencies with conservative politics does not fit the social conscience of the black churches. The highest percentage of students from minoritized racial and ethnic groups in mainline Protestant seminaries is African American. Mainline schools have become more attentive to African American students and have more African American faculty than the others. They have advanced critical race theory in theological education more than any other group of schools. Some schools have been stalwart advocates for diversity, inclusion, and justice with their church bodies and have actively pursued antiracist efforts in their own institutions.

The descriptions of racial/ethnic populations of theological schools do not define the realities of individual students from minoritized groups. Most theological schools have predominantly white student bodies and faculties, which makes students and faculty of color racialized minorities. Most of these students and faculty must navigate a minority status in a white majority culture.[48] The twentieth-century effort to make the normative level of theological education postbaccalaureate meant that communities of color that have had more limited opportunities in higher education have been denied admission even if the school is proud to admit "qualified" persons regardless of race. This is part of the reason that Hispanic/Latino/a enrollment is as low as it is. The white culture of most theological schools requires students of color to learn not only the theological subjects but also the culture of the school, and to become adept at code switching to thrive in school and in the contexts they will serve—most often in a racial/ethnic community of faith.[49] For example, white culture, in general, does not deal with community and family in the way that many communities of color do, and that can make a Hispanic student's reticence about pursuing graduate education for family reasons less understandable to a white professor encouraging that student to undertake doctoral study. In the same vein, the desire of an African American with a newly minted PhD to pursue research that addresses the needs of the African American community can seem less important to a white-dominated tenure and promotion committee than research in other areas.

The issue of race in religion and American theological education is like almost no other issue. The persistence of prejudice, the devastating effects of racism on communities of color, and the inability to find remedies that make the culture and all its people whole combine to make it the problem that does not go away. Addressing it breeds fatigue, as small successes are followed by failures large and small. Yet with resistance to this fatigue, commitment to stay the course, an increase in the number of faculty and students from historically underrepresented groups in theological schools, and continued efforts to resist racism, theological schools can address this American original sin.

The future for American Christianity in this century will be defined by persons of color, and if present trends continue, persons of color will constitute the majority of students in US theological schools within two decades. The story of race was dominant in the history of theological education in prior centuries but was kept in the shadows. In this century, it will be in the spotlight. Virginia Theological Seminary made news in 2019 for being one of the first US institutions of higher education to establish a reparations endowment fund to compensate heirs of slaves who helped build its main administration building, to support African American Episcopalians, and to support efforts to ameliorate the ongoing effects of racism. It is a start. More theological schools need to come to terms with the racist issues in their past and present if they hope to make it to the future.

Religion, Culture, and Higher Education as Dominant Influences in Theological Education

A new country shaped by newly invented democratic ideas and a disinclination to reproduce Europe fashioned its own culture. Religion contributed to shaping that culture. Over time, however, it appears that culture had more shaping influence on religion than religion had on culture. The Protestantism of the nineteenth century enjoyed a cultural privilege that, although not formally established, contributed to the development of a model of professional theological education that had not existed in England or Europe. This quasi establishment of white Protestantism created the need for a Roman Catholic subculture, which defined Catholic life until World War II and isolated its theological schools both from Protestant theological schools and from the broader community of American higher education. The privilege the culture had extended to white Protestants was withdrawn in the latter part of the twentieth century, necessitating painful adjustments to a nonprivileged status. Considerable evangelical energy was devoted to the culture wars in the last decades of the century. Whether producing culture, enjoying the privilege of the culture, being isolated and segregated by cultural conventions, precipitating a religious reaction to a cultural reality, or adjusting to the loss of cultural privilege, religious communities and theological schools have been shaped by culture in substantive ways.

While theological education and higher education began in the colonies as a common enterprise, they began to be separated in the nineteenth century. Theological education moved to freestanding schools, and the colleges and universities founded for religious reasons in colonial America, for the most part, abandoned ministerial education. Although separate, Protestant theological schools organized their work in ways similar to how colleges and universities organized theirs, began academic guilds at about the same time, used pedagogical practices like those of other higher education institutions, and developed accreditation practices of quality assurance. They tended to follow the lead of the broader community of higher education. The nineteenth century saw the formation of publicly funded colleges and universities, and by late in the century, the ascendancy of the research university. Higher education has influenced theological schools directly in the form of educational practices and institutional forms.

Religion has historically influenced theological schools. They were founded from religious visions and serve religion's purposes. When Christianity grows, new schools are founded. When it declines, existing schools are merged or closed. Religious movements often result in the founding of theological schools, but even the most effective work of these schools seldom results in religious movements. Education for Catholic priests differs from education for Protestant ministers not because Catholic faculty think differently than Protestant faculty but because priestly education is embedded in the church and follows papal declarations and episcopally approved norms. Evangelical schools are suspicious of intellectual work not because their faculties have problems with it but because the religious communities they serve do. Theological schools are derivative institutions; they do not exist for their own purposes; they do not do their work only in the ways they decide to do it; they do not have a mission apart from the religious communities they serve; they are not masters of their own fates; instead, they are inextricably bound to the fates of religious communities.

The history of theological schools in the United States, at least as I read it, demonstrates the powerful influence of culture, higher education, and religion on the institutional forms and educational practices of theological schools. These influences have affected all the streams of theological education discussed in this chapter, and I think they will affect the next theological education just as profoundly.

Interlude

This book is about the "next" future of theological education in the United States. The first chapter suggested that the future will not likely be a linear continuation of the current practices of theological schools. Nor is it going to be something completely different. Though dominant practices will continue, the next theological education will look and feel different, at least in some ways, from what it has been in the past few decades. I focused in the second chapter on the history of American theological education in order to explore a hypothesis that the institutional forms and practices of theological schools have been shaped by cultural, educational, and religious forces. From my reading at least, the history supports the hypothesis. These forces have shaped theological education in the past and will shape the next form that theological education takes. While future forms of theological education may be discontinuous with the past, the influences that will shape these new forms and practices are continuous.

This raises a significant question. Is theological education simply the victim of these influential forces? If it is, the next theological education will be whatever these forces determine it to be, and there is no reason to lay out the contours of the next theological education. If it is not the case, then how do these influences influence?

For the most part, the success of theological education in the past was not because external influences determined that it would succeed or because theological education somehow turned these powerful forces in the directions needed for success. I think theological schools in the colonies, in the era between the Revolutionary and Civil Wars, in the era between the Civil War and World War II, and in the most recent era after World War II succeeded because they found a way to fit with the cultural and religious moments that came and went during these eras. They did not so much "fit in" the times as they "fit with" them. The prevailing expressions of theological education during each of these eras were "right" for the cultural moment, the state of religion, and the practices of higher education as they existed in each historical moment.

The authenticity of theological education in the future will depend on how well theological schools fit with these three powerful influences. Whether theological education gets it right or not will depend on how well it perceives the dominant cultural, religious, and higher education influences and adjusts its work to fit with them. The schools cannot change the cultural moment or prevailing practices in higher education. They have less power to change religious practices than they would like to think. The schools' task will be to discern the shape of these dominant influences as this century matures in its third and fourth decades, and to shape their work in the context of those influences. The schools have a choice. They can continue doing what worked well in another cultural and religious moment but may not work as well in the current moment, or they can reinvent their work to fit the current religious, cultural, and educational realities. Chapter 3 proposes a goal for the next theological education, and chapter 4 discusses the educational practices this goal will require. For both chapters, it is crucial to understand that formational theological education, as I am proposing it, is the combination of educational goals and practices. Both are essential and deeply interrelated.

Formational Theological Education and Its Goals

For a bishop, as God's steward, must be blameless; he must not be arrogant or quick-tempered or addicted to wine or violent or greedy for gain; but he must be hospitable, a lover of goodness, prudent, upright, devout, and self-controlled. He must have a firm grasp of the word that is trustworthy in accordance with the teaching, so that he may be able both to preach with sound doctrine and to refute those who contradict it.

—*Titus 1:7–9*

Now a bishop must be above reproach, married only once, temperate, sensible, respectable, hospitable, an apt teacher, not a drunkard, not violent but gentle, not quarrelsome, and not a lover of money. He must manage his own household well, keeping his children submissive and respectful in every way—for if someone does not know how to manage his own household, how can he take care of God's church? He must not be a recent convert, or he may be puffed up with conceit and fall into the condemnation of the devil. Moreover, he must be well thought of by outsiders, so that he may not fall into disgrace and the snare of the devil.

—*1 Timothy 3:2–7*

This chapter opens with two texts. The two texts have their problems—the relationship of contemporary religious leadership to the elders or bishops who oversaw fledgling house churches in the first century, the use of these texts to assert male-dominated religious leadership, the culturally removed counsel about marriage and keeping children submissive. But the texts remain instructive about characteristics fundamentally important for persons who would lead communities of faith—"temperate, sensible, respectable, hospitable, an apt teacher, not a drunkard, not violent but gentle, not quarrelsome, and not a lover of money"—

Positive Views of the Honesty and Ethical Standards of Clergy, by Religion

Please tell me how you would rate the honesty and ethical standards of people in these different fields—very high, high, average, low, or very low? How about clergy?

■% Catholic   ⋮⋮% Protestant

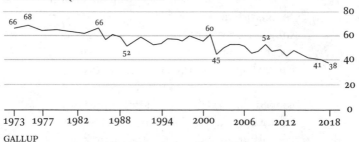

% High/Very high
GALLUP

Americans' Confidence in "the Church or Organized Religion"

■ % Great deal/Quite a lot of confidence

GALLUP

the kinds of qualities that are not bound by time or culture. Now compare these two texts to the two charts on p. 76. The charts have their problems—the validity of answers that people give to callers over the phone, the reductionism of forcing perceptions about reality into categorical response possibilities. But the data over time do paint a picture of a declining positive view of the ethics of clergy (a drop of more than 20 percentage points in the past fifteen years) and declining confidence in organized religion (a drop of almost 30 percentage points from 1975 to 2018). These data are the product of sophisticated polling strategies, and even after accounting for margins of error, the decline in these polls remains striking. Is there any chance these texts and charts have something to say about the next theological education? This chapter addresses that question by reflecting on theological education in the current cultural moment. I argue for a mode of theological education that stresses *formation* and try to assess that goal in relation to the factors that have been so important for theological education throughout its history: the church, the wider culture, and higher education.

Theological Education and the Current Cultural and Religious Moment

In the era of colonies and early nationhood, the education of ministers was not distinct from the education of civic leaders, and educated clergy sometimes served in both roles. In the modern age of the late nineteenth to early twentieth century, with the growth of urban industrial centers and many congregations, theological education upped its educational standards. By the mid-twentieth century, theological education took the form of professional education with its focus on skills as well as specialized biblical and theological knowledge. Throughout this long period, religion enjoyed a privileged place in the culture and religious participation was generally high.

For the past several decades, however, the social location of religion has been changing, and the data in the Gallup charts above reflect that change. Many reasons undergird this decline in the social influence and cultural esteem of religion, in addition to the moral and legal failures of religious leaders that have grabbed headlines. While a certain kind of religion has been publicly present, evident in recent elections, researcher Robert Jones has shown that it is beginning to abate and will likely continue to shrink in the coming decades because of demographic changes. According to reliable data from the Pew Forum on Religion and Public Life, the percentage of Americans attending services of worship has been declining. The fastest-growing religious identification in the United States has been "no religious affiliation" (more than 20 percent of the US population), and for several generations the religious participation of generational cohorts has declined. While religious participation in the United States remains higher than that in any other liberal democracy, the changes afoot are neither transitory nor ephemeral. These shifts constitute the cultural context in which to discern the future of theological education.[1]

Theological education has changed and continues to change, but it changes slowly, as I have already noted, and it tends to change by accrual rather than by replacement. Theological schools keep much of what they have always been doing while they add options. Over time, they shed some but not all of the old, and they lean into the new, but not all at once. They do not change by replacement, but they do change. In the past decades, *how* the schools taught was changing, and for Protestant schools, *where* they taught was changing as well as *when* students could study. But, for the most part, *what* the schools have been teaching has remained quite stable. It was a curriculum that emerged in the nineteenth century and matured in the twentieth century into the model of professional theological education that exists today. This curriculum and educational model developed during an era of strong religious institutions and robust denominational structures. What should be the pattern of theological education when these realities are no longer present?

I argued in the first chapter that theological education seems to be between the times. Perhaps that has always been the case.

The education of priests and ministers has always existed, from ancient New Testament qualifications for ministry to current religious practices and structures. If it is always at least somewhat between the times, then theological education never gets it "right" for more than a season. What is good at one time—responding effectively to a fixed scriptural point and a transitory cultural moment—can be bad for another time. I think the current cultural moment calls for renewed attention to the enduring qualities enumerated in the above Scriptures: being not violent but gentle, a lover not of money but of goodness, not quarrelsome but prudent, upright, devout, and self-controlled. As religion is increasingly on the defensive and many religious institutions are in decline, an invaluable response will be to ensure the fundamental Christian character of Christian leaders. That emphasis on character will require the next theological education to assume more responsibility for cultivating these qualities in ministerial candidates. This effort will change parts of the curriculum and some of the strategies related to teaching and learning. Language of "parts" and "some" might not grab attention in our cultural moment. This is a time that relishes overwhelming change and is fascinated by the one event that can purportedly change everything, even though that is seldom the way things actually work. Changes to "parts" and "some," however, can precipitate a surprising transformation.

The name I propose for the "next" theological education is "formational." The 1996–2018 accrediting standards of the Commission on Accrediting of the ATS use "formation" in at least two ways. The introduction to the standard on curriculum, for example, states that "A theological school is a community of faith and learning that cultivates habits of theological reflection, nurtures wise and skilled ministerial practice, and contributes to the formation of spiritual awareness and moral sensitivity."[2] In this usage, "formation" is limited to spiritual awareness and moral sensitivity. The standard continues that "the curriculum should be seen as a set of practices with a *formative* aim—the development of intellectual, spiritual, moral, and vocational or professional capacities—and careful attention must be given to the coherence and mutual enhancement of its various elements" (emphasis added). In this usage, "formative" applies to the curriculum as a whole, not just to spiritual awareness and moral maturity. My proposal for formational theological education will include these elements, along with others, and give particular attention to the process of theological education.

Roman Catholic schools use "formation" as the primary name for education that prepares candidates for the sacrament of ordination. Not sharing this sacramental understanding of ordination, most Protestants have been leery of the term. Roman Catholics have also been comfortable with the implication that "formation" suggests a specific outcome of a process; Protestants also object to the notion of a prescribed outcome. Even with these hesitations, in recent years different groups of Protestants have begun to talk of formation more frequently.

William Sullivan called this emphasis on formation a distinctive feature of theological education. Sullivan, then at the Carnegie Foundation, oversaw a series of studies on education for the professions, including clergy, engineers, lawyers, physicians, nurses, and others. He notes that at the center of the pedagogy for the education of clergy is "the idea of formation: the recognition that teaching and learning are about much more than transferring cognitive facts or even cognitive tools. Learning in the formative sense is a process by which the student becomes a certain kind of thinking, feeling, and acting being." Sullivan continues: "Although seminaries have not escaped the power of the technical model of professionalism, the intellectual core of their teaching has been a concern with the significance and practical implications of the interpretation of texts, customary practices, and experience. The focus of which has kept the idea of formative education alive."[3] With dynamics like these in mind, I use "formation" as a name both for a particular kind of goal for theological education *and* for the educational processes that goal requires.

I think that the present cultural moment is calling theological educators to make explicit what has been assumed, to accept responsibilities for areas that have been minimized in theological education, and to expand its focus to the wide range of characteristics that will give ministry the authenticity it needs in this culture at this time.

The Goal of Formational Theological Education

The place to begin exploring the goal of formational theological education is in the tradition of Christian thought. Edward Farley noted that, in the Middle Ages, theological study was understood to result in a *habitus*, "a cognitive disposition and orientation of the soul, a knowledge of God and what God reveals,"[4] which reflects an Aristotelian concept of knowing as an "orientation of the soul." Theologian David Kelsey has argued that the aim of contemporary theological education should be to understand God truly, and that the theological concept of "wisdom" is one of the ways in which Christians "understand." He goes on to note, however, that "wisdom obscures important differences" that include "contemplation, discursive reasoning, affections, and actions that comprise a Christian life."[5] The goal of theological education should begin with careful attention to these two observations. Such education should be about a *habitus*, an orientation of the soul, and should understand that a wisdom of God and the things of God is a kind of understanding that embraces many ways in which an individual comes to know God, such as contemplation, rational discourse, and actions.

Theological education found its way to the colleges in the American colonies as the study of divinity. Farley noted that divinity as studied in early America was "not just an objective science but a personal knowledge of God and the things of God in the context of salvation." It "was an exercise of piety, a dimension of the life of faith."[6] The study of divinity was required of all students in those schools, not just students studying for ministry, but as education for ministry separated from general higher education, the "study of divinity" fell into disuse.

What goal would attend to *habitus*, to Christian understanding with its many characteristics, to the concept of the study of divinity that intermingled Christian commitment and knowledge, and to the formational educational practices that theological education brought to its version of professional education? The goal that I propose attends to these but with significant additions. Farley's and Kelsey's descriptions are broad, but they focus on the cognitive and intellectual, with some leaning toward the affective. I want to increase the affective elements and include stress on a range of behavioral elements, including those that constitute the practices of ministerial leadership. Farley argued that one of the problems with theological education (by which I think that he meant the professional model) is that it has become too clerical in orientation. My proposal assumes that the practices of clerical ministry are themselves formative; they are a way in which pastors and priests come to an orientation of the soul. As a result, I propose a goal that assumes that cognitive, affective, and behavioral elements are all important, perhaps equally important.

The goal of theological education should be the development of *a wisdom of God and the ways of God, fashioned from intellectual, affective, and behavioral understanding and evidenced by spiritual and moral maturity, relational integrity, knowledge of the Scripture and tradition, and the capacity to exercise religious leadership.* This definition is an awkward and technical effort to get at something that is far more ineffable. The awkward and technical aspects can be elaborated while the ineffable aspects can only be respected and affirmed.

Wisdom of God and Ways of God

Wisdom refers not to an accumulation of knowledge or capacity for good judgment but to longing for or love of God, a participation in divine life through the ongoing promptings of the Spirit. While this is an essential part of Christian life for any believer, it takes on special importance for one who serves in ministry. The past decades of theological education have rightly and consistently made the point that a minister is not necessarily someone who is more spiritual than other Christians, and certainly cannot be "more" Christian on behalf of people who are "less" Christian.

While this emphasis humanized religious leadership, it may also have undervalued how important ministers' love for God is—both for their own spiritual lives and for their authenticity as religious leaders. It is as wrong for people in the pews to assume that their pastor loves God on their behalf as it is for a pastor to assume that his or her love of God is irrelevant to authority to serve as a leader. The love of God is experienced or expressed in many ways. It is "traditioned"—it takes different forms and expressions in different communities of faith. The wisdom of God that a Pentecostal minister experiences and expresses will be different from that of a Roman Catholic priest, but neither can be an authentic leader without a wisdom—without loving and longing for God. This longing is not a guarantee that dark nights of the soul or periods of doubt will not occur; indeed, it is frequently their cause. Loving and longing are about aspiration more than achievement, about maturing more than maturity.

Wisdom in the ways of God comes through relationship, not just from information. It is, for example, by loving a spouse over many years that one becomes wise about a spouse's ways with sadness and joy, about what the spouse most cherishes and hopes for, about how the spouse forgives and makes it through dark moments. In a similar way, wisdom of the ways of God grows out of having longed for and loved God. The spousal example fails in a significant way because spousal wisdom is personal. Wisdom of the ways of God is communal. It reflects an accrual across the centuries and cultures in which people have loved God and shared some account of their love. Any one individual's perception is inadequate, even vacuous, absent the wisdom of the community. The communal nature of wisdom of the ways of God is one reason that learning is central to Christian life and authentic ministry.

Fashioned from Intellectual, Affective, and Behavioral Understanding

To the extent that the wisdom of God and the ways of God are learned, it is a learning fashioned from intellectual, affective, and behavioral patterns of knowing. While each is different, each informs and contributes to the others. I may be moved by a hymn tune, for example, but moved even more when the text to that tune fits it aesthetically and intellectually. In this case, the intellectual (text) adds meaning to the affective or emotive (tune). I may know a passage of Scripture well, understand it, but then hear it set to music. When the beauty of the music explicates the meaning of the text, the result is new understanding. Most people who attended Sunday school as young children learned songs that were often accompanied by physical motions. Some of these songs linger in memory long after childhood because they combined intellectual ways of knowing (learning the words) with behavioral ways of knowing (making the motions), and, because the songs were fun for children to sing, they involved affective ways of knowing, as well. These illustrations would be misleading if interpreted to say that cognitive, affective, and behavioral modes are only means of learning. They are not. They are about something more. They are about "understanding," in Kelsey's terms. Each pattern of learning contributes to a form of understanding, and none is superior to the others.

Intellectual understanding is ubiquitous in theological education. A large share of the effort of theological learning is devoted to intellectual effort—books are read, papers are written, discussions are engaged in, languages are learned—that constitutes the center of current practices of theological education. Eleventh-century theologian Anselm famously expressed what he understood as a paraphrase of Augustine, that theology is "faith seeking understanding." Few introductory theology classes conclude without some mention of this enduring definition. How the character and ways of God are understood influences how the Christian faith is constructed and perpetuated. Ideas matter.

Decades ago, my daughter and I were walking home from her preschool. The weekend before, the youth and children of our congregation had performed Benjamin Britten's *Noe's Fludde.* Our daughter had been captivated by the story, the music, and the children dressed as animals. Somehow our conversation turned to that production and the story of Noah and the flood. I asked her about it. She explained that people had been bad, and God got angry and caused a flood that killed the people. I was taken aback. Her idea about the flood was somewhat right but altogether wrong. The story is about justice and judgment, but it is not about a God who throws a temper tantrum. Justice is an intrinsic part of divine love, and if she thought that God was a God of anger, her nascent faith would have little chance of maturing to embrace a God whose ways are love and justice, mercy and grace. Intellectual understanding is at the "heart" of Christian faith.

If intellectual understanding is at the heart of Christian faith, there must be an understanding of the heart—an affective understanding. If Anselm's motto is the most used for understanding the intellectual work of theology, then Pascal's must be the most-used statement about affective understanding: "The heart has its own reason which Reason does not know; a thousand things declare it."[7] The writer of 1 John is rather passionate about the importance of the affective in Christian life: "Beloved, let us love one another, because love is from God; everyone who loves is born of God and knows God. Whoever does not love does not know God, for God is love" (1 John 4:7–8). Love is a way of *knowing* God; love provides an understanding of God that is not possible in other ways. The text makes the interesting point that we grasp love's understanding of God not in mystical meditation but in the act of loving others. The human ability to love is a gift of God, and as God's gift, it reflects part of God's own identity. When people love one another, they discover in themselves something of the character of God—they experience a replica of God's most central characteristic, and the result is a kind of understanding about the ways of God that could be achieved by no other means.

Learning the ways of God also engages human behavior. When a surgeon performs a complex procedure on an open body, or an adult rides a bicycle for the first time since childhood, or I strike the keys on the computer keyboard writing these words, the memory seems to be in the muscles—the behavioral element of the actions. The memory is actually in the brain, of course, but a different kind of memory is involved in behaviors than the kind that remembers facts. Behavior can provide its own form of understanding. A congregation sponsors a mission trip, for example, and the youth travel to an area that has been damaged by a flood or tornado. For a week, they clean, carry debris, or make minor repairs to buildings. They come back to their congregation and report how they see their faith differently. In worship, most people bow their heads for prayer and some lift upturned hands in supplication during the Lord's Prayer. People kneel in worship in some Christian traditions while in others they lift their hands in praise. While these religious behaviors vary by Christian tradition, most traditions engage particular behaviors in acts of worship or service. My hunch is that religious communities have learned these ritual behaviors because what people believe is tutored by what they do: behavior brings a form of understanding that is different from intellectual or affective ways of understanding.

The *wisdom of God and the ways of God*—this longing for and loving of God, this understanding that accrues from the centuries and cultures that people have longed for God—are *fashioned from intellectual, affective, and behavioral understanding*—these very different ways of comprehending, leaning into, and learning. The goal of theological education, however, is not the joy of knowing God and the things of God, satisfying as that may be, but *spiritual and moral maturity, relational integrity, knowledge of the Scripture and tradition, and the capacity to exercise religious leadership.* Like intellectual, affective, and behavioral understanding, these are integrated and interactive qualities that inform one another and contribute to a whole that differs from the sum of the parts.

Spiritual and Moral Maturity

A paragraph is a poor vehicle to convey centuries of thought about the nature of Christian spirituality and the fabric of moral maturity. Some images point to these long traditions, but they are not those traditions. Some faculty members at a seminary where I taught for twelve years tried to define Christian spirituality and concluded that it "involves transforming responsiveness of the whole person individually and corporately to God, the 'Beyond in our midst,' and participation in God's continuing creation and redemption in and through Jesus Christ."[8] This is certainly not a better definition than a hundred others, but it is sufficient for consideration at this juncture. Spiritual maturity emerges from a three-way intersection where the human longing for God meets the mystery of God and the work of God in human lives. The ways people love God are traditioned, and the way spirituality is experienced varies by tradition. Mature spirituality is different for a Quaker who regularly participates in an unprogrammed meeting than for an Episcopalian who regularly attends service with music, homily, and Eucharist. While there are common elements—the responsiveness to God and participation in the things of God—those elements can be experienced and expressed differently.

Definitions of moral maturity are no less abundant than definitions of Christian spirituality, and often vary by the psychological, philosophical, or theological perspectives on which they are based. Whatever else, moral maturity includes a theologically informed understanding of right and wrong, the intellectual capacity to discern moral issues in human and community contexts, and the ability to behave in ways that are consistent with the determination of what is right and what is wrong. The decline in confidence in the ethics of clergy in the Gallup data that introduced this chapter appears to be related to the public moral failure of clergy through sexual misconduct, the sexual abuse of children, the use of power to obtain sexual attention, and the theft or misuse of charitable funds. It is likely that these clergy knew right from wrong but failed to act rightly in the context of their knowledge. Other times, knowing the right thing to do can be more subtle and nuanced, and failure to do the right thing is in part a failure to understand what the right thing is. Doing the right thing also can be difficult because, once the right thing is discerned, it can be daunting to do. All these difficulties mean that moral maturity is a goal, something to be learned by working on it. Moral maturity is not easy and does not come as a free gift. In Pauline language, "that I would, I do not, and that I would not, that I do." Moral maturity is at the heart of the public credibility that makes moral witness possible and undergirds the authority of religious leadership. Moral and spiritual maturity contribute to many of the qualities deemed appropriate for religious leadership in the texts cited from the Pastoral Epistles—qualities like "above reproach," "not a lover of money," and "not violent but gentle."

Relational Integrity

A religious leader can be spiritual and moral and still be relationally immature or inappropriate. Qualities like "temperate," "sensible," and "hospitable" are aspects of relational integrity and may or may not result from spiritual or moral maturity. Relational integrity includes taking others seriously and attending to them, treating people with kindness and patience, cultivating the capacity to empathize, attending to how others see the world and interpret its meaning, and exercising relational flexibility. Sometimes a good pastor is described as someone who has a "pastor's heart," and that description likely reflects the qualities that I have associated with relational integrity. Leaders who adjudicate difficult pastoral transitions in which the congregation perceives the pastor to have been at fault often cite the pastor's "difficulty at getting along with people" as a contributing factor to the conflict. Relationships matter. The God of Christians is a relational God, and communities of faith are intrinsically relational. Relational integrity is not about being a nice person or likable, as good as those qualities might be: it is about embodying and enacting a faithful way of being human.

Knowledge of Scripture and Tradition

The Pastoral Epistles also require the leader (the bishop) to "have a firm grasp of the word that is trustworthy in accordance with the teaching." Christianity is a content-rich tradition. Its founder was a first-century rabbi known for his teaching and knowledge of texts. He interpreted the law in a way that cut to its underlying principles and made of a mustard seed and olive tree lessons of deeper religious truth. In an era of limited literacy, Jesus's first followers wrote books to document his teaching and mighty deeds, and the first major interpreter of the Jesus movement, Paul the apostle, provided intellectually adept guidance for Christianity in its first century and beyond. The early church fathers wrote sermons and works of theology and practical guides for life, and by the fourth century the church had reached consensus about the books that would form the New Testament. The tradition continued; monasteries preserved and reproduced Scripture and other writings, and theological understanding grew. The printing press was invented, and the Bible and theological books became available to an increasingly literate world. The Reformation— the many reformations—brought more books that enlarged the tradition as well as the kinds of persons who could study it. The Enlightenment gave impetus to the reasoned analysis of the accrued and accruing tradition. The tradition has continued to the present moment, rich in every way, expanding its library and deepening its perception of the human condition and the hope of God for the human family and God's world. This text and this tradition—Scripture, theology, history, the languages of the Bible, ethics —provide a rich and varied array of "the word that is trustworthy in accordance with the teaching." It is incumbent on persons who desire to lead communities of faith or who represent themselves as Christian leaders to know this tradition that has been loved and debated, defined and redefined, interpreted and reinterpreted across cultures and centuries.

The Capacity for Religious Leadership

The Pastoral texts also identify two other ministry skills: the bishop should be an "apt teacher" and "be able . . . to preach with sound doctrine." Preaching and teaching have been central in the life of the church since its beginning. The arts of ministry—the skills that provide the capacity for leadership—are not content-neutral. Good preaching is not just an oratorical event: it is an act of communicating the Christian story ("sound doctrine" in the language of the text). Good teaching is not merely about pedagogical excellence: it is about instructing people in the tradition. The range of ministerial skills has increased over the years, especially in the past century or so, to include leadership and administration, pastoral care and congregational studies, organizational theory and sociology of religion, and others. The list has been growing and likely needs to continue to expand. The issue of cultural and congregational literacy—being able to read a community and congregation or parish—is becoming more crucial to effective leadership. Like teaching and preaching, these areas have a theological core, combine into an overarching field of pastoral theology, and constitute something different from the mere borrowing of knowledge from other domains.

The goal of theological education is a wisdom of God and the ways of God fashioned from intellectual, affective, and behavioral understanding and evidenced by spiritual and moral maturity, relational integrity, knowledge of the Scripture and tradition, and the capacity to exercise religious leadership. Perhaps this aim of theological education should include more, or perhaps stating the aim in these terms is too idealistic. Regardless of its possible problems, it is altogether reasonable to assume that the aim of theological education is directly linked to the qualities that are important for persons who serve as Christian leaders.

Assessing This Goal in Terms of Religion, Culture, and Higher Education

I argued in the second chapter that theological education is influenced by the church, with its tradition and current needs; by higher education, with its changing practices over time; and by cultural moments, with their undulating variations. If these influences are as strong and consistent as I have suggested, then they also provide a basis for assessing the integrity of the goal of theological education.

Does This Goal of Theological Education Serve the Church's Tradition and Current Needs?

Many of the expectations embodied in this goal—particularly those related to spiritual and moral maturity, relational integrity, knowledge of Scripture and tradition, and some of the skills that ministry requires—were first identified in the passages quoted earlier from the Pastoral Epistles. They emerged early in the church's life and continue to be important. While ministry has had and continues to have dark periods in which power, social structures, and human sinfulness prevail, and while ministry has had and continues to have its charlatans who abuse the human longings that prompt people toward faith, these failures, malfeasance, and abuse point to the enduring integrity of these expectations for good and faithful ministry. The church and the gospel it declares are magnified by the presence of these qualities and diminished by their absence.

The adequacy of this goal might also be judged by the current hopes of people of faith—a kind of reader-response assessment. What would the persons who receive the ministerial and priestly efforts think of this goal for the education of the people who bury their parents and baptize their children? Would these qualifications reflect the "holiness" parishioners hope for in a Roman Catholic priest? Would they invite the confidence of a Baptist congregation in its pastor or seem suitable for an executive minister responsible for the area cooperative ministry with its housing and food-support programs? Would a mainline Presbyterian congregation respect a learned clergyperson who embodied these qualities? Would an evangelical megachurch consider these qualities to be winsome in its pastoral leaders? A reader-response evaluation would be inappropriate if all it did was provide a consumer-dictated sense of ministry that may be popular but does not respect the church's long tradition. It might prove appropriate, however, if leadership must be received in order to be effective.

More than four decades ago, I was the junior member of a research team asked to identify characteristics considered important or detrimental to the practice of ministry. The study was conducted with the assumption that laity, parish clergy, seminary professors, chaplains and counselors, and judicatory officials could legitimately express the church's perception of qualities important for ministers and priests. More than five thousand clergy and laity across the spectrum of denominations represented by ATS member schools in the early 1970s were asked to respond to five hundred statements about ministry.[9] The survey was readministered to smaller but still substantial populations of laity and clergy fifteen years later, and then another fifteen years after that, with remarkably stable ratings across three decades. In the final analysis, the expectations embodied in the responses could be distilled into three fundamental affirmations: (1) ministers or priests must love God—expressing that love in ways that vary with different traditions' understanding of the ways in which God is loved and evidenced in characteristics such as moral integrity and spiritual sensitivity; (2) priests and ministers must love the people they are called to serve—particularly with evidence of the disciplines of loving others such as respecting them, keeping confidences, being available to serve when the people need them, attending sympathetically to the wounds and brokenness of others; and (3) ministers and priests must be able to do the work of ministry—knowing the texts and tradition and performing the tasks of ministry with dependable skill. If these are legitimate expressions of the church's desire in a more modern moment, then this goal of theological education fits both the long tradition and the current moment.

Does This Proposed Goal Reflect Realities of the Current Cultural Moment?

This is an era of suspicion of many social institutions, but the critique of religion and religious leaders seems especially acute in its fundamental questions about the value of religion and the trustworthiness of religious leaders. A model of theological education focused on the proposed goal would not change the cultural perceptions that are derived from many influences, but theological education in this American century cannot be faithful without some attention to the publicly declining perception that clergy can be trusted to act ethically and that the church can be trusted as a custodian of the common good. The church and its leaders will not be able to address this cultural perception with still more knowledge, more ministerial skill, or newly conceived approaches to ministry. Addressing it will require emotional maturity, moral integrity, and unimpeachable ethical standards.

Another way current cultural reality speaks to this goal is in the reconsideration of competence and smartness. Edward D. Hess and Katherine Ludwig argue that the "new smart" needed in business and other social arenas redefines being smart as "excelling at the highest level of thinking, learning and emotionally engaging with others that one is capable of doing."[10] While "thinking" continues to be a part of their definition of "smart," it is no longer enough in a future when artificial intelligence will be able to do much of what "smart" people have done. The new "smart" must include the ability to continue learning and "emotionally engaging with others," qualities necessary for collaboration and teamwork. Would it not be interesting if the highest form of human attainment in this century of artificial intelligence were relational and emotional as well as intellectual? What if relational integrity and emotional maturity—qualities that have always counted in ministry—emerge as the qualities most needed for commerce and innovation in the most advanced democracies? If this proves to be the case, part of theological education's role at this time and in this culture will be to maximize those abilities in candidates for religious leadership.

Does This Proposed Statement Reflect Questions or Issues in Higher Education?

Higher education may pose the hardest test for the integrity of this proposed goal for theological education. I wrote previously that theological education has tended to adopt higher education practices, which certainly was the case from the nineteenth through the mid-twentieth century. Theological schools grew out of what we would call liberal arts colleges, and in many ways shared common educational goals to cultivate character and civic consciousness in persons who would serve a common good. Over time, things have both changed and stayed the same. David Kelsey writes about theological education as occurring between Athens and Berlin.[11] Athens is the metaphor for *paideia*—a kind of education that nurtures the soul. It is about character, values, and the kind of learning that prepares people for service that contributes to a common good. Berlin is his metaphor for the modern research university, which originated in the founding of the University of Berlin. It was a form of education with Enlightenment energy and a focus on the generation of new knowledge and objective rationality. Early American colleges were "Athens" in their educational goals, as was the theological education they housed. During the nineteenth century, the Berlin pattern of education began influencing American higher education, and theological schools used both models.

The Berlin model gained increasing supremacy in higher education in at least two ways. The first was in the rapid growth of publicly funded institutions. Before the Civil War, higher education in America was primarily in the form of private liberal arts colleges or teaching universities. After the war, many public institutions were founded, and a century later, the vast majority of undergraduates were enrolled in public institutions. The Berlin model was invented for publicly funded higher education in Germany, and it was readily adaptable to the growing number of publicly funded institutions in America. While these schools had the goal of educating for the common good, it became increasingly difficult in the twentieth century for them to educate in *paideia* ways because of the pluralistic character of the American population and the prevailing perspective that most value-laden decisions were private and individual issues rather than common and corporate.

The second way in which Berlin gained ascendancy was in the emergence of the research-intensive university. These universities—both public and private—understand their commitment to the common good in terms of scientific advancement and generation of new knowledge. Research-intensive universities are a dominant influence in American higher education because they educate a significant number of faculty in all of higher education, are perceived as the leadership institutions, and how they do their work influences how faculty think academic work should be done.

Liberal arts colleges have held on to the educational goals of *paideia*, but the humanities, which were the primary carriers of this goal, have come under increasing suspicion, fueled by the perception that liberal arts education does not prepare graduates for employment upon graduation. To argue that theological education needs to be even more attentive to the educational goals that are clearly aligned with *paideia* education, as I have argued in this chapter, is counter to the dominant pattern of intellectual work in the university.

Learning to love God does not lend itself to the kind of objectivity that is most valued in some forms of higher education. Learning to love God involves substantial intellectual requirements, but objective rationality is not one of them. Rational objectivity requires testing truth claims, and the most truthful claims of Christianity are not readily testable. The focus on the generation of knowledge places high value on discovering something new, and some of the most important tasks of religion are to assert something quite old. This intellectual moment is suspicious of grand narratives, and ultimate grand narrative claims are at the center of religious reality. These binary comparisons wither, of course, as most binary constructions do in a multidimensional world, but they illustrate the problem my proposal has if it is to be advanced in current and emerging intellectual tools of higher education.

Research-oriented higher education has the perfect tools for one kind of knowing, but formational theological education requires different tools. The study of religion is a case in point. To have a home in the university, theological education needs to use the academy's intellectual tools, and to use those tools, religious studies courses tend to explore the phenomena of religions—tracing their practices and history, identifying similarities and differences among traditions, assessing religions' cultural presence and impact, identifying ways that people of different religions can talk with one another, and so on. These are important and honorable intellectual efforts, but they are not designed to lead a student to love God more or to be more devoted in his or her faith. My point is illustrative and hypothetical, but it remains a point. The goal of formational theological education will require substantial and careful intellectual and educational work, and while that work will use many of the dominant tools of higher education, it will require other tools as well.

The changes that occurred in higher education in the twentieth century have not gone unnoticed or without critique. James Burtchaell asserts that the religious foundations of American colleges and universities have been surrendered to a perception of higher education where objectively neutral rationality dominates.[12] Mark Schwehn has argued that higher education has left the religious foundation in which it largely began, and as a result, suffers from the loss of values that are central to scholarly work.[13] Critique is not the only effort at this point. An interesting set of essays edited by Douglas Henry and Michael Beaty provides proposals to renew and restore education that claims a goal of moral or character formation.[14] Some liberal arts colleges are working to reestablish their historical *paideia* pattern of education through programs like the Network for Vocation in Undergraduate Education, which was "formed to enrich the intellectual and theological exploration of vocation among undergraduate students."[15] This network of more than 250 predominantly liberal arts colleges uses the word "vocation" to mean different things, but all member schools are using curricular and cocurricular efforts to help students think about meaning and purpose in their lives—educational goals reflecting the *paideia* model. The concern is not just in the liberal arts colleges. In the most recent changes to the requirements for baccalaureate degrees at Harvard, students must complete at least one course in the area of ethics and civics that "engage[s] with large questions about right and wrong, helping students grapple with the nature of civic virtue and the ethical dimensions of what they say and do."[16]

The proposed goal of formational theological education would be supported from the perspective of the church and its needs at this time and would address worries in the culture about religion and its leaders. It would also have a home in the parts of higher education that attend to civic virtue, meaning and purpose in life, and educating for a common good. It could increasingly become a stranger in the parts of higher education whose absolute commitment is to objectivity, rationality, and the generation of new data. Theological education will continue to have part of its identity in higher education but may need to forge other parts of its identity outside the dominant intellectual and educational practices of the most elite levels of higher education.

The Formational Goal and Current Educational Practices in Theological Schools

Let's assume that this goal or aim of theological education is appropriate for church, culture, and at least some segments of higher education, and let's assume that religious leaders who embody the qualities to which this aim is directed would be perceived as competent and trustworthy. Let's assume that these qualities are faithful to the church's long tradition and embody qualities of leadership that are truly Christian. Let's assume that theological schools affirm these qualities and would be pleased if their graduates reflected them. If these assumptions hold, then one might expect theological schools to bend their educational efforts toward this aim.

Is that the case? As best I can tell (with apologies to people who prefer clear lines and straight answers), the answer is both yes and no.

Protestant theological education attends to some of these qualifications exceptionally well while it does not attend to others. And while Roman Catholic theological education attends to all of them more fully, it is still learning how to do this well.

What are the schools doing well and what are they doing less well? Consider the proposed goal one more time. Most theological schools, especially Protestant schools, are effective educators for the parts of the goal set in italics and less effective for the parts set in roman type in the following restatement: "The goal of theological education is a wisdom of God and *the ways of God fashioned from intellectual*, affective, and behavioral *understanding* and evidenced by spiritual and moral maturity, relational integrity, *knowledge of the Scripture and tradition, and the capacity to exercise religious leadership*."

Theological schools, with their courses and degree programs, along with the organization of scholarship with its disciplines and faculty specialties, provide the kind of theological education that educates students well in *the ways of God fashioned from intellectual understanding and evidenced by knowledge of the Scripture and tradition and the capacity to exercise religious leadership*. Most schools can demonstrate that students have learned about the ways of God, that they know a great deal about Scripture, that they have a good intellectual understanding of the church's tradition and their particular part of that tradition, and that they have a good understanding of the tasks of ministry and how to perform them. While theological schools devote considerable educational space to learning the tasks of ministry, a school, because it is a *school*, is still better at teaching theology, history, and Scripture, because those areas are learned in the traditional liberal arts patterns of study and schools are structured and organized in ways especially well suited for that kind of learning. A student may learn to love God more, or become more morally or spiritually mature, or come to terms with the way some of his or her personal characteristics influence the practice of ministry, but these results are often an indirect consequence of theological studies. Most of the courses that seminarians take do not identify these kinds of goals as the primary outcomes.

The part of the proposed goal at which Protestant theological education is less effective is the kind of learning that contributes to *a wisdom of God fashioned from affective and behavioral understanding and is evidenced by spiritual and moral maturity and relational integrity.* While these qualities often do emerge from the study of theology, Scripture, and tradition, they are typically not the enumerated educational goals in those courses. Roman Catholic schools in the United States, by contrast, attend to these areas and expect candidates for priesthood to be prepared for the sacrament of ordination with evidence that these qualities have reached a certain level of maturity. If theological schools value these characteristics and consider them appropriate if not mandatory for Christian ministry, why don't they give explicit attention to them in their educational efforts? I think this inattention occurs for several reasons. Some of them are related to perceptions about education, others to the characteristics of students, and still others to issues in the educational practices.

Perceptions

The first perception is that it is not explicitly the job of theological schools to address these areas. Christian faith is nurtured over time and in many communal contexts. A person who has grown up in church, for example, has likely had experiences in activities like Sunday school, confirmation classes, retreats, service events, mission trips, worship, and even leadership of worship in a community of faith. College years offered additional opportunities to learn and grow in religious sensitivity through campus ministry events. Together, these events, activities, and practices would have provided a wide ecology of support, nurture, and religious instruction that contributed to many of the qualities identified in the proposed goal. The role of the theological school is not to duplicate the tasks that other parts of the ecology can provide but to offer what is needed but less present in those other parts, like substantive intellectual grounding in theology, Scripture, and history. The president of one ATS member school recently said theological education is "about becoming an educated person, knowing the traditions, being able to think critically, being able to express your thoughts."[17] This president is not even sure that theological education is about the cultivation of ministry skills. From this perspective, the primary job of a theological school is intellectual engagement with text and tradition. Schools can't do everything that needs to be done, so stewardship requires them to provide what they do best and what the church and world most need.

The second perception is that while moral and spiritual maturity, relational integrity, and the deep longing for God may be important qualities for ministry, they simply can't be taught in a school. They may be learned, but they are learned over long years, through the experiences and vicissitudes of life, through the moral insight of others, and through dark nights of the soul. This perception is not so much "It's not the school's job" as "Schools simply can't do this job." It does not protest the importance of these qualities for ministerial leadership but argues that they simply cannot be learned in a theological school. Because they are important qualities, the church must assume responsibility for certifying ministerial leaders who give evidence of them. Ultimately, communities of faith must bear the responsibility for certifying the presence of the "gifts and graces" that the church perceives as vital, even when there is no clear indication of how and where those gifts and graces are learned.

Students

Achieving the formational goals described above is also difficult for reasons related to students, especially the current generation of students.

First, this formational goal might be redundant because many current seminary students—unlike previous generations—have already received intensive formation. While the age of students varies widely, and some schools have much younger student bodies than others, in the 2018–2019 academic year there were as many students over fifty enrolled in ATS member schools as there were students under thirty. The overwhelming majority of all students are over thirty years of age, and if these desirable qualities emerge from experience and the work of the Spirit of

God over time, then these students are already "formed"—the developmental aspects of spiritual or moral maturity have already occurred. The theological school can provide a review of these qualities and has a basis for critiquing inadequate versions of them, but the key teachable moment has passed. The students may not be old dogs who can't learn new tricks, but life may have contributed to a formation in faith that does not need to be re-formed in a theological school. In fact, the reason so many students are coming to theological study later in life may very well be the result of the spiritual, moral, and relational maturity they have developed. They have worked in other areas, learned hard lessons, contributed as volunteers to the ministry of their parishes or congregations, and, in their experience and maturity, found a call to ministry. Students coming to theological schools with more developed spiritual, moral, and relational sensitivities do not need a repeat of this kind of formational education. These students most need the scriptural and theological content to be preachers and teachers and the technical skills to perform the tasks they feel called to undertake.

Another issue with the current generation of students relates to the interdenominational quality of many Protestant schools. I mentioned earlier that Christian spirituality is traditioned—it takes particular forms in different Christian communities, with no generic pattern that transcends all those communities. Few theological schools any longer have students from only one denomination. Many do not even have a majority of students from one Christian family. In these schools Unitarian-Universalists, Pentecostals, Anglicans, Baptists, and historic black church members are all preparing for ministry together. While this diversity provides multiple educational benefits, it makes it difficult to educate all students in the particularities of their own communities. One of the reasons Roman Catholic schools may provide better education in terms of the proposed goal is that all MDiv students are Roman Catholic, and while the Roman Catholic community as a whole is far more diverse than any one Protestant community, the homogeneity among students and presumed educational outcomes provide deep and meaningful particularities. Schools might find ways to educate formationally across Christian families—they have found, for example, ways to teach different structures of ecclesial polity—but it will require considerable effort. The existence of a rich diversity of ecclesial traditions undoubtedly has a formational impact on students. But if that impact is to form people for faith and ministry, it will require deliberate educational attention.

Educational Issues

Some current educational realities make parts of the formational goal difficult. One of these is the increasing variety of degree programs. While the master of divinity continues to have the largest enrollment of any degree offered by ATS member schools, fewer than half of all students are taking the MDiv. Most are enrolled in one of more than two hundred different degree programs offered by ATS member schools. The formational goal defined in this chapter is not appropriate for all the degree programs offered, which leads to an important qualification. This next future of theological education contains two divergent paths. One is the kind of education that pastors, congregational ministers, and other ordained or rostered leaders need, and the other is the kind needed by persons preparing for ministry-related professions like counseling or social work that do not require ordination, or by persons studying theological disciplines for academic purposes. The "next future" focuses on the first of these paths. While most of the history of American theological education has been about the education of pastors and ordained ministers that serve in a variety of church- or parachurch-related roles, that educational center of gravity has weakened, and this call for a formational pattern of theological education is, among other things, a call to give particular attention to the education of ministers and priests who will serve as religious leaders and spiritual guides in an increasingly secular future. The formational goal for the students in the second track, however, is still relevant. Such students have chosen education in a theological school, and likely understand their professional specialty in terms of their Christian vocation. The most fundamental formation, as Ted Smith points out in his volume in this series, is formation in faith, and that kind of formation uses all the tools I am advocating for formational theological education.

Another issue is the culture of higher education. Although some forms of higher education have affirmed patterns of formational effort with undergraduates, like attention to vocation in undergraduate education mentioned earlier in this chapter, the emphasis on research and generation of new knowledge that is ubiquitous among research-intensive institutions may not be particularly hospitable to formational patterns of theological education. Divinity schools in research universities have a responsibility to serve the broader university research goals, and this can consume the energy necessary for the kind of formational education I am proposing. In the culture of the research university, noble as it is, producing graduates who are lovers of God and the ways of God will not be valued if the divinity faculty is not also producing the research that will advance theological scholarship. These sophisticated communities of scholarship, of course, can and do provide formational education.

I was interviewing students at a divinity school located in a research university, and a student said that she could tell her friends in other theological schools that her teachers wrote the books her friends were studying. I am not sure what her comment implied about formational theological education—bragging rights might not be formational routes—but it did reveal the power of a theological education with faculty who are intellectual leaders in their fields of study.

The current structures of theological education developed as the religious ecology was strong and most students had been a part of it; as the culture included religion more centrally, even privileging it; and as religious institutions were robust in many ways. These structures cultivated the development of schools and scholarly disciplines that have contributed to more understanding about Scripture and tradition than at any other time in the history of the church, as well as to developments that expanded instruction in the pastoral arts at a time when the tasks of ministry were proliferating and the need to do these tasks well was increasing. Much has changed since this structure was developed, and what has been good may not be as good in the context of the changing social location of religion, the degree programs that students want to pursue, the students who attend theological schools, and regnant values in higher education.

The Next Future of Theological Education

Theological education has received many critiques in the last few decades. As the church has struggled, theological education has been blamed for causing its problems or enabling them to persist. Some of these critical analyses have come from outside theological education, such as from leaders of successful megachurches, and some from inside, such as from former professors who bemoan new emphases or educational strategies. The critiques are accompanied with proposals for the next theological education, which range from abandoning it altogether, to returning it to some former glory, to changing it in fundamental ways. My critique is not that current forms or practices are a failure. It is that they reflect a particular cultural moment, a certain time in the life of American churches, and that moment has changed. The coming moment calls on theological schools to emphasize some things that have been present but in the shadows, for them to do some of the things the church used to do so there will be a future in which the church might be able to remember its task. The way that theological education has been done, sophisticated and valuable for one day, is not adequate to the tasks required by a new day.

Miroslav Volf and Matthew Croasman have assessed the current influence of theology—broadly defined to include all the disciplines that constitute the curriculum of theological education—in the academy and culture. "Theology has no spectacular new insights to offer, nothing analogous to mountain ranges on dwarf planet Pluto or the genetic basis of certain cancers; there are no stunning new tools to whose design theology has contributed, nothing analogous to a driverless car or the material magic of graphene." They lament that in the modern university that thrives on discovery of new knowledge, the core of theological studies has lost its audience and reputation. Volf and Croasman argue that it is partly the fault of the commanding dominance of science and technology and partly the fault of theology remaking itself into a more objective, science-like area of study to compete in this intellectual world. They propose that theology pursue its purpose "to discern, articulate, and commend visions of and paths to flourishing in light of the self-revelation of God in the life, death, resurrection, exaltation, and coming in glory of Jesus Christ, with this entire story, its lows and its highs, bearing witness to a truly flourishing life." Theology has not always been understood as having its purpose related to a "truly flourishing life," and in an era of prosperity gospel and frail claims about "flourishing," it needs substantive explication, which their argument provides. Volf and another collaborator, Justin Crisp, contend that part of the renewal of theology entails a recovery of the union of what the theologians teach and the life they lead, or at least aspire to lead. The "execution of the central theological task requires a certain kind of affinity between the life the theologian seeks to articulate and the life the theologian seeks to lead." Later, they write: "It would be incongruous for theologians to articulate and commend as *true* a life that they themselves had no aspiration of embracing."[18] Christian pastors and other religious leaders are theologians in the way that Volf defines theology, and while their focus may be the parish and the world rather than the university, it would be equally incongruous for them to preach what they do not aspire to live.

Theological education has assumed the importance of the character of the Christian life for the Christian leader, with its dimensions of a wisdom of God that is more about loving God than about accumulating information about God. It has assumed the importance of spiritual maturity. It has never doubted that moral maturity is crucial to the practice of ministry and knows firsthand that relational integrity is crucial to the complex patterns of ministerial work. Theological schools are smart enough to know that learning comes in more than one way, and that deep religious learning en-

gages more than the head. The task for the next theological education is to take seriously what theological educators know and to
cultivate the institutional and educational patterns that will give
preference to underdeveloped aspects of theological education.

Theological education has had many futures, and I think its next
future will need patterns of education that are as intellectually
rigorous and pedagogically sophisticated as present patterns,
but that also take seriously and responsibly a wider vision of the
aims and purposes of theological education than the current
model has embraced. The next future of theological education
will not be completely different from the current version; schools
will need to use the tools they have already developed, recover
some patterns of education they have allowed to go dormant,
and continue to do some of what they are doing. But they will
also need to imagine a larger arena in which theological education does its work. The next future of theological education will
concern itself with the content of theological studies, the skills
needed for ministerial leadership, *and* the spiritual, moral, and
relational character of Christian life to which religious leaders
should aspire. It does not give itself permission to exclude any
of these areas.

4

Formational Theological Education and Its Educational Practices

> I think and write about religion because I am
> religious. It occurred to me early in life that
> I wanted to align my life with things that
> seemed true to me.
>
> —*Marilynne Robinson*

While I was working on this manuscript, I spent a week at St. Meinrad Archabbey and Seminary, a Benedictine community that I have visited occasionally since the early 1980s. I stayed in an apartment near the seminary wing, attended prayers in the abbey church, and took most of my meals with the students. These students were studying for the priesthood amid revelations of criminal sexual abuse by priests as well as the failure of episcopal leaders to respond appropriately. Certainly, they talked about that. But they were more interested in sharing with me stories of God's call in their lives, their hopes for ministry in a repentant and renewed church, and of course, their attempts to make sense of metaphysical philosophy and dogmatic theology. They were able and committed, like most of the seminary students I have known.

These students were being formed for the ministerial priesthood in a very particular way. They attended classes together, ate meals together, attended chapel together, left the quiet of the campus for work in parishes across southern Indiana one day a week, and spent most evenings studying in the library or their rooms. They were single men studying full time for a celibate priesthood. Each had a spiritual formation director, worked with a human formator, and was evaluated annually by faculty and formation staff. Reports of their intellectual and spiritual growth, their development of pastoral skills, and their human formation are submitted to their sending bishop or superior. Their MDiv requires four years of work, which many prepare for with two years of study in philosophy. For most of these students, their sponsoring dioceses or religious institutes cover the cost of their education.

A few years before I retired from ATS, I visited a new seminary in the Wesleyan tradition founded by Indiana Wesleyan University. The university had a strong on-campus undergraduate program and was known across the Midwest for its adult degree completion programs, first in extension centers but more recently through Internet-based distance education. The seminary was an applicant to ATS and had utilized all the allowances for distance learning that the ATS accrediting standards permitted at the time. The curriculum was designed so that the core courses were taught online, almost always by more than one faculty member, and in a way that combined traditional theological disciplines so that, for example, New Testament, theology, and one of the pastoral arts might be covered in one course.

Students participated in cohort groups throughout the academic year and came to campus for weeklong intensive sessions. They took elective courses that were typically taught by a single professor and focused on a single discipline. The admission standards for this program required students to be working at least half time in some ministry context. Students came to know one another both online and in person.

I interviewed a group of students who were just completing the MDiv offered in this way, and it was obvious that they knew one another well and had supported one another over the past several years through family illness and difficulties in their congregations and other ministry contexts. These students praised the program. Many were employed full time in ministry, and this program had given them the chance to go to seminary. They learned a great deal and felt as though they had grown as Christians and as ministers.

I recently attended a graduation service at Pittsburgh Theological Seminary, where I serve on the board of directors. Students who had completed certificate programs were recognized, and the master's and DMin students were granted their degrees. It was a celebratory moment following years of hard work. These graduates had also been prepared for ministry in a very particular way. Some had studied full time and completed their MDiv degree in three years; most required more years because they took less than a full load each semester to balance study, work, and family responsibilities. A few had lived on Pittsburgh Seminary's very urban campus during their study; most had not. All had been on campus for their courses, because the seminary did not offer online courses. Most had attended chapel services if their courses began or ended around time for chapel worship. They had been taught by a faculty with considerable academic expertise, many with national reputations, each having written books, several of them many books. All the graduates had been intellectually stimulated and academically educated. Many had participated in some global engagement event in Cuba or the Philippines or elsewhere, and most had worked at least part time in congregations or church-related nonprofits. Each student had been evaluated by the professors whose courses he or she had taken, and each had received a good version of traditional theological education. Of the three schools I have mentioned, the theological education this school provided was most like the one I received fifty years earlier. Classes were smaller than the ones I had, required readings and course syllabi were quite different, and much more attention was given to the educational outcomes of the courses and degree programs, but the structures and pedagogical practices of this theological education were remarkably similar.

The goal for theological education I proposed in the previous chapter was that graduates would acquire *a wisdom of God and the ways of God fashioned from intellectual, affective, and behavioral understanding and evidenced by spiritual and moral maturity, relational integrity, knowledge of the Scripture and tradition, and the capacity to exercise religious leadership.* Ask any of the students at St. Meinrad or Indiana Wesleyan or Pittsburgh if their studies resulted in the attainment of this goal, and I think they might demur. Ask if they think they have been changed by their theological education, and I think almost all would say yes. If these students were changed by their theological education, then the formative power of theological study was present, even if the goal was not completely attained. While some similarities exist in the ways they were educated, the overall educational models their schools used were dramatically different. They were educated in such different ways, in fact, that whatever goal of theological education they attained or whatever change they experienced could not have been a function of a particular educational practice or model. What is the relationship of this formational goal to educational practices?

Educational Goals and Practices

If the primary question of the previous chapter was, "What should be the goal of the next model of theological education?" then the primary question of this chapter is, "What educational practices will that goal require?" In many ways, the second question is tougher than the first. Educational proposals always come with problems. Whether intentionally or not, for example, a new strategy can be proposed with so much energy that it leads people to think it is the only method that will contribute to attaining the goal. Or proposals for new educational methods are often seen as replacing older, less effective methods. A third possibility is that proposals for educational strategies can be overly precise, in which case the proposal is insufficiently expansive to accommodate complex educational goals. The opposite can happen, as well, as proposals can be too generic, in which case they become more theories of practice than strategies for practice. This list is not exhaustive, but it illustrates some of the problems that can emerge from a set of educational proposals. I think my proposals avoid the first three but probably not the fourth. Theological education is diverse and becoming more diverse, and a set of concrete proposals will not work. My proposals will be too general for some readers, but hopefully they will reflect the movement necessary to get from an educational goal to the educational practices that implement it.

As I have noted more than once, formational theological education is already occurring in a variety of ways. The Roman Catholic education at St. Meinrad takes an intentional, formational approach, based on the norms of the *Program of Priestly Formation* (see chap. 2) that require educational attention to pastoral, intellectual, spiritual, and human formation in the context of a residential community of study, worship, and life.[1] Indiana Wesleyan has structured theological education so that students' primary community is the ministry they are serving, and the formational strategy at this school centers on tightly integrating ministry practice and study. At Pittsburgh Seminary, a primary formational strategy is the content of theological studies. The academic study of Scripture is not the same as the devotional reading of Scripture, but Scripture has a way of speaking its truth no matter how it is studied, and as students discover that truth, they are shaped religiously as well as intellectually.

In all three schools, still another form of formational energy is present: the motivations that bring students to seminary. Year after year, new students are surveyed about their motivations for entering ATS member schools. Among the most common is a sense of God's call in their lives.[2] Students go to a theological school because they sense that God has led them, and that calling makes them open to being shaped in faith as they respond to their call. Formational education occurs for many reasons, in many ways, with and without educational intent and design.

This chapter explores practices that are an integral part of formational theological education. Some fit easily into the current shape of many theological schools, some emphasize using current practices in a slightly different way, others require different educational approaches, and still others require new institutional understandings. While some of these changes are subtle, others constitute a tall order. I present them in four broad categories that relate to the work and commitments of faculty and the perceptions and practices of theological schools: institutional vocation and faculty faithfulness; commitment to educational goals and assessment of learning; attending to spiritual maturity and relational integrity; and making the institutional changes that a formational model will require.

Institutional Vocation and Faculty Faithfulness

A formational educational model does not begin with specific educational practices; it begins with a renewed sense of the vocation of the theological school and the faithfulness of faculty for that vocation. This is a startling first order of business. Yet if a school is to cultivate a wisdom of God and the ways of God that is more than acquisition of information about God, it is a necessary starting place.

Institutional Vocation

Much of the work of a theological school is practical: recruiting students, finding money, providing educational experiences, making large and small decisions that constitute a system of governance, and more. The reason for the work is missional: educating people toward wisdom of God and the ways of God; providing the context in which people learn to behave and feel as well as to think and reflect; being a seminary—a seedbed— where people learn to pray and relate rightly to others. The most important educational strategy of any seminary is pursuing its mission with passion, clarity, and integrity. If a school does not know what its mission is or does not give itself passionately to the attainment of that mission, educational strategies will accomplish very little.

How a school does its work has educational and even forma-tive power. In the professional model of theological education, the competence a school exhibited in its practices was a pedagog-ical practice. If the goal was to have students attain professional competence in their ministry, then the seminary teaches that, at least in part, by exhibiting professional competence in its work. In formational theological education, the fidelity of the school to its religious mission has a similar effect. In the professional model, students could ask: If this school can't competently keep my bills straight or schedule classes efficiently, how can it teach me to be a competent minister? In a formational model era, stu-dents could ask: If this school doesn't care about its religious vocation, then how can I learn a wisdom about God?

A research project several decades ago asked theological schools important questions about their core values and how they educated toward those values. Some of us involved in that project began asking about the "soul" of the school. Schools don't have souls, of course, but our question was a sociological way of asking if a school's religious identity was serious enough for stu-dents to perceive it and researchers to identify it. Did the practices and institutional habits of the school reflect its religious identity as a *theological* school, or was its identity primarily as a *school* whose educational efforts and degree programs were focused on preparation for ministry? No theological school, of course, would say that it does not have a religiously formed identity, but some schools are more conscientious about that identity than others. Most of the schools founded before World War II, for example, were founded by denominations, and their religious mission was embedded in the denomination for which they served a func-tional role. As such, their religious identity was often derivative of the denomination's core religious identity. As denominations have waned in power, and as many schools have become decid-edly less denominational, these schools can no longer claim their religious vocation via the proxy of their denominations. They will need to cultivate some of these habits or practices of the non-denominationally affiliated schools founded later in the twentieth century. If I am right about the kind of theological education that is needed in the future, theological schools will need to steward their theological and religious identity carefully, cultivate institutional practices and disciplines that sustain that identity, and reflect that identity in their educational practices.

Faculty Faithfulness

If faculty are to teach students in a formational way, then they need to attend to the intrinsically religious aspects of their intellectual and pedagogical labor. One can teach the content of Christianity in a less than Christian way, but one cannot do so if the goal is Christian formation.[3] What might be considered a Christian way of teaching? I think it involves certain virtues and careful stewardship of intellectual effort.

Mark Schwehn contends that intellectual work in higher education depends on virtues that have both significant functional importance and deep religious roots. Most of Western higher education developed as a Christian enterprise, and as long as the academy was situated in the context of a religious foundation, the motivations for and nurture of these virtues were part of the general fabric of an institution's religious identity. Even though most of higher education has separated from its religious roots, these virtues remain important. The problem is that they have been exiled from the religious contexts that cultivated them. Whether the educational context is religious or not, these values are crucial to the integrity of intellectual and pedagogical practices. Schwehn writes that "so long as the activities of teaching and learning involve communal questioning in search of the truth of matters, the exercise of virtues such as humility, faith, self-denial, and charity will be indispensable to higher education."[4] When these virtues are present in intellectual and educational efforts, they comprise a "spirited inquiry," in Schwehn's words. Faculty faithfulness is not about personal piety but is about spiritually informed virtues that undergird intellectual and educational practices.

Humility is a central Christian virtue. It begins with a sense of honesty about oneself and what one can and cannot do, and the resulting understanding of dependence on God, one's culpability in sin, and need for God's grace. It is also necessary for all kinds of learning because learning begins with an individual's perception that he or she has something to learn. A lack of humility is a dominant characteristic of know-it-alls who are unaware how little they know. Schwehn notes that humility entails the "presumption of wisdom and authority of the other." Humility is self-referential in that the individual is aware that he or she does not know something that needs to be learned, and it is other-referential in that the individual is aware that somebody else knows it. Learning cannot occur apart from intellectual humility.

Faith is indispensable in Christian life. According to the Scripture, we are saved by faith, but it seems an odd virtue for scholarship, with the central demand for critical thinking and testing evidence in higher learning. Schwehn's argument, however, is that scholars "rely upon the work and thought of others, and we cannot possibly think well in an atmosphere of mistrust." Scholarship requires asking hard questions, but it also requires trusting good sources, and this is an act of faith. For Schwehn, intellectual life requires us to believe "what we are questioning and question what we are believing . . . we believe in order to understand."[5] Faith is not the enemy of critical scholarship but a requirement for it.

Self-denial has a long history in the Christian tradition. John the Baptist declares that Jesus "must increase, but I must decrease," and Christian spirituality is full of disciples who have gone to the desert, sacrificed life or personal pleasure for a common good, or denied themselves in one way or another. Self-denial is also a necessary intellectual virtue. Schwehn says, "we must be prepared to abandon some of our most cherished beliefs. And we cannot do this unless we have to some extent cultivated the virtue of self-denial, the capacity first to risk and then to give ourselves up if necessary for the sake of the truth."

Finally, and the greatest in the Pauline hierarchy of virtues, is charity. Charity in teaching and learning means avoiding the erection of "straw man" arguments and belittling others to prove a point. It means embracing other persons and their ideas as worthy of respect. Schwehn illustrates this value as a historian: "I think that the exercise of charity toward my historical subjects is bound to make me a better historian: more cautious in appraisal, more sympathetic with human failings, less prone to stereotype and caricature."[6] Charity is an educational virtue, as professors take students seriously, respect their humanity, treat them with respect, and hold students accountable with demand and compassion.

Other virtues may be critical, but I agree with Schwehn that these four are central and uniquely critical for formational theological education. To the extent that faculty exhibit humility about what they know and don't know, about what can and can't be known; to the extent that they treat students, colleagues, and the content of their disciplines faithfully; to the extent that they demonstrate the ability to devote some of their own time and ideas in service to others and a greater truth; to the extent that they love the content that they teach and the students to whom they teach it—to this extent they are teaching in a formational way. Student character is nurtured by faculty character. These virtues do not require a drumroll or spotlight; they are formative by their very nature. And they are fundamentally Christian.

While theological schools are not the only places where the church does its thinking and faculty are not the only crucial thinkers for its work, schools and faculty do provide an invaluable resource for the intellectual mission of communities of faith. This mission requires careful stewardship, and stewardship involves practices in which faculty should engage.

The first is a broad understanding of the kinds of learning that formational education requires. Intellectual effort informs, corrects, and elucidates. But other ways of knowing—like behavioral and affective ways—are equally necessary. Intellectual ways of knowing are not superior to these other ways of knowing. If faculty act as if their intellectual ways of knowing are primary or superior to other ways, then students will be discouraged from pursuing some of the learning they need for effective service in the coming decades.

Another formational practice for faculty is stewardship of their intellectual agendas. In higher education in general, and especially in theological education with its limited dependence on external grants for funding, the agenda for research and exploration of new knowledge tends to be the personal choice of a scholar. Theological faculty often take their cues for research from the intellectual agenda in their scholarly guilds, but perhaps they should attend instead to the intellectual needs of communities of faith. The great gift to the church of intellectual effort is minimized if theological educators focus their energy on issues that are distant or irrelevant to the needs of ecclesial communities.

These practices, like most of the recommendations that I make, should not substitute a new thing for an existing thing, like the church's current agenda for the one dominant in an academic guild. Rather, faculty should ensure that the intellectual needs of the church are included in the overall scholarly agenda. These intellectual needs include translating ancient religious affirmations into the intellectual idiom of the day, providing a continuing intellectual foundation for the church's work in the future, and teaching communities of faith what they most need to know, which may not be what most intrigues the church at any one moment in time. Faculty faithfulness includes the intellectual effort to examine critically what is studied, not just performing a critical study of whatever piques researchers' fancy.

Commitment to Educational Goals and Assessment of Learning

For the past several decades, theological schools have given considerable attention to the educational goals of courses and degree programs. Goals were always present, in one way or another, but they were more often assumed than articulated, and efforts to articulate them often evoked more disagreements and discussion than most faculty members care to remember. Over time, however, goals have achieved more educational substance than the public relations claims of many institutions. The change came, as it sometimes does in the Christian tradition, accompanied by "kicking and screaming," but nonetheless theological schools joined the rest of higher education in the contested age of goal identification and outcomes assessment.

The issue of goals was contested, true, but assessing the attainment of those goals was even more contested. Even as agreement on goals was reached, it was sometimes lamented that the goals most desired in theological education were not assessable, and the demand for assessable goals meant that the school would need to settle for less. The result was, at times, an exercise in educational casuistry in which the goals identified were the ones that could be assessed rather than the goals that were most desired. A goal of "formation" could be justifiably rejected because it is too ineffable and not readily assessable. The learning that future religious leaders most need, however, should not be dismissed simply because it is difficult to assess. Schools need to be clear about the kind of formation they hope to offer students and then about reliable signs that that formation is happening.

Commitment

A broad formational goal like the one I have proposed will have its greatest chance of attainment if the institution and its faculty are truly committed to nurturing a "longing for God . . . fashioned from affective and behavioral understanding . . . and evidenced by spiritual and moral maturity and relational integrity," among the other qualities identified in the overall goal. Commitment provides the motivation necessary to order curricula and educational efforts toward the goal and develop the assessment strategies the goal requires.

Institutions need commitment because this goal may require some schools to make institutional changes and develop new partnerships, especially with congregations and other ministry contexts. Most schools have limited resources, and any proposal that adds to the cost of educating religious leaders will be challenging. The costs associated with this proposal are not great, but they will still require institutional commitment to utilize limited funds, institutional energy, and time.

Faculty commitment is needed because the goal is addressed classroom by classroom, course by course, experience by experience, and achieved only by the individual and corporate efforts of the faculty. The corporate effort, however, may be more difficult. Doctoral education in most theological disciplines is intensely personal, often solitary. From early in their training, faculty learn to work alone. Commitment to corporate goals is something that most scholarly work does not tutor, but it will be needed if the expansive goal of formational theological education is to be attained. This goal will require the school and its faculty to understand the changed cultural reality the church faces in the future, and to order their individual expertise toward a shared commitment to educate students for that changed social location of the church and its ministry.

Assessment

These days in higher education, an educational goal cannot exist without some strategy for assessing the way in which and the degree to which it is attained. For theological schools, assessment is not so much a technological educational practice as it is an act of stewardship. It is stewardship of the financial costs of providing theological education to students; it is stewardship of the expense that students incur to become theologically educated; and it is stewardship of the service that religious leaders provide to communities of faith. Little value is gained by teaching the best of theological content if no student ever learns it. My former colleague at ATS, Debbie Creamer, writes that "assessment works when we do it out of love, curiosity, and stewardship—not out of bureaucratic obligation, out of defensiveness, or to appease external audiences."[7] Assessment out of love, curiosity, and stewardship is the only kind that, in the end, will prove useful for formational theological education.

The question is how to properly assess the formational goal I have advocated. The more complex an educational goal, the more subtle and difficult its assessment. The proposed formational goal is very complex. Good assessment is possible, however, and many of the pieces are already in place. Schools, for example, already know how to assess the intellectual learning of biblical/theological content and the ability to think critically about it. Tests and papers, class presentations and participation in discussions are all commonly used. Assessment of outcomes like spiritual and moral maturity and relational integrity is more difficult, but practices are in place for even these areas. A joint project of the former Seminary Division of the National Catholic Educational Association and the ATS Commission on Accrediting, *An Assessment Workbook for Roman Catholic Seminaries* contains chapters on assessment of human and spiritual formation.[8] Another effort, the Seminary Formation Assessment Project, funded by the John Templeton Foundation and directed by David Wang, is developing, testing, and exploring longitudinal implications of a sophisticated instrument to assess spiritual development. The ATS has been working with theological schools for almost two decades to cultivate patterns of assessment for theological learning, and the ATS website now has scores of articles about processes, resources, case studies, and strategies for the assessment of learning. These more modern efforts follow the varied practices by which Christian communities have sought to assess spiritual maturity of candidates for religious leadership, from the process of selecting the abbot of a monastery, to the questions of ordination councils of a small Baptist congregation, to the discernment in silence of Quaker decision making. So, whatever the demands of assessment for this formational goal may be, the schools are not starting with nothing.

To assess this goal schools will be required to work on issues they may not have developed previously, and while different schools will work in different ways, some guidelines may be helpful. The primary instruction from the ATS Commission on Accrediting about the design for assessing educational outcomes is that it be simple, sustainable, and sufficient.[9] Another is that good assessment is not limited to quantitative information. When ATS committees were considering changes to descriptions about assessment a decade ago, they adopted the language of "discernible" outcomes rather than "measurable" outcomes for specifically this reason. A love of God, for example, may be discernible even if it is not measurable. Still another guideline is to assess the comprehensive goal. Assessment of parts of a goal is often easier than assessment of the entire goal, but a degree is granted based on attainment of the goal as a whole, and schools should keep this comprehensive goal always in mind.

If this formational goal were proposed twenty years ago, with a similar assumption about needed assessment, the task would have been all but insurmountable. Theological schools, however, have learned a great deal about assessment, and as a result more knowledge and resources are now in place to implement appropriate assessment. The assessment of this formational goal of theological education will still be difficult, even with this knowledge and these resources, and strategies will take both effort and care.

Educating for Spiritual and Moral Maturity and Relational Integrity

The practices I am proposing for formational theological education privilege issues related to spiritual maturity, moral maturity, and relational integrity. While these issues are crucial for ministry in the present cultural moment, they tend to be the least attended elements in current practices. Some educators have assumed they are related, and that mature spirituality, for example, will result in moral maturity and relational integrity. That does not seem to be the case. Forty years ago, the ATS convened a seminar on the issue of character and theological education, at which George Lindbeck, an esteemed theologian of that era, presented a paper contending that "spiritual maturity is different from the psychological and moral varieties. . . . The spiritually mature are sometimes inferior to the immature . . . in the cardinal moral virtues of prudence, justice, courage, and temperance despite their eminence in the theological virtues of faith, hope and love."[10] More recently, Marvin Oxenham has argued that theological educators should "keep the language of spiritual formation and character formation separate."[11] Both scholars are right. Spiritual maturity, moral maturity, and relational integrity are different domains of being human and Christian, and they are best attended to as related and at times overlapping domains, but each requires its own particular attention.

Spiritual Maturity

Jewish educator Hanan Alexander describes Rabbi Akiba's ancient response to the question whether the study or the practice of the Torah is more important: "study is more important because it leads to practice." Alexander summarizes ways in which this response can be interpreted and concludes, "the study of Torah is a form of spiritual practice, and the practice of its precepts is a form of study. Study celebrates divine love and enriches the practice of God's commandments. Practicing them deepens our grasp of their meaning in our lives. This understanding is reinvested in sacred study that yields new insight and, in turn, enables practice to become more joyous." Alexander argues that study in this way avoids the perception of education as an instrumental activity that leads to an outcome because "it leads to practicing the very vision of goodness being studied, it is an end in itself."[12] Spiritual maturity is not the educational outcome of an educational process.

If theological schools cannot educate students to spiritual

maturity, is it appropriate to hold them responsible for spiritual growth, as the formational model of theological education I have proposed does? Yes, if spiritual maturity is an important aspect of ministerial or priestly service and theological schools claim to prepare people for these roles. If they are responsible, how should the work be done? The most common ways schools have addressed this issue in the past may not be sufficient for the attainment of a more fulsome formational goal. Efforts related to spiritual growth have often been relegated to covenant or peer groups, chapel worship, or what students discover about themselves in ministry contexts. These activities are not wrong, nor should they be abandoned, but they are not enough. The subjects that theological schools teach have an intrinsic formative power, but the way they are taught—as a form of graduate professional education—can fail to exploit that power.

Consider the study of sacred Scripture. Almost a third of the typical theological curriculum is devoted to study of Scripture, but it is usually focused on content and critical methods for study. Can the study of a sacred text nurture spiritual growth? I think the answer of the church through the ages has been yes, but the academic study of the texts may be insufficient. The texts warrant critical study, and both individuals and communities of faith benefit from it. In the end, however, sacred texts have been written, assembled, and passed down because they point toward an ultimate goodness that shapes human lives. Learning these texts is incomplete if it is not influenced by the goodness they teach. The academic study of Scripture is the starting point in a theological school, but could it not be accompanied with the invitation to let the text form the learner as a religious person? This invitation will require the prompting of the professor, the willingness of the student to live into the text, and sufficient time for students to let the text stir their souls.

Or, consider the study of homiletics. It occupies a much smaller part of the theological curriculum and is only one of many areas of the pastoral arts, but it provides an interesting opportunity for formational education. Homiletics courses typically include study of communication theory and introductions to great sermons and various sermon styles, but most classes focus on preparing sermons and delivering them to the class or some other group, which is typically followed by oral or written evaluation. Preaching a sacred text, however, has a way (or at least should have a way) of shaping the student preacher's own faith. Perhaps, after a student has rightly addressed the evaluations of peers and professor, the student could be encouraged to reflect on why the text was chosen, what it means to the student, and how preparing and delivering it and then reflecting on its evaluation influenced the student's faith.

These examples, inconsequential as they are, illustrate what I wrote earlier about faculty intentionality. Theological education is spiritually formative, but that formation can be enhanced by a kind of teaching and learning that deliberately calls attention to the ways theological learning for the work of ministry is also theological learning for the life of faith. This intentionality does not change the curriculum or cost a fortune, but it can contribute to a more formational education for ministry.

Whatever spiritual formation is, and however it matures, students need to process what is going on in their lives, talk about their doubts and faith, and reflect on their fears and longings. Many theological schools provide structures or persons who can help with this processing or discernment. All Roman Catholic schools educating candidates for the ministerial priesthood, for example, provide spiritual direction every year of students' theological education. Some Protestant schools also provide structures or individuals to help students discern and grow in their spiritual journey. These strategies, unlike the ways courses might contribute to spiritual reflection, do add cost. Yet if ministerial leadership will be even more dependent on the minister or priest's spiritual maturity in the future, then the cost of not attending to students' spiritual growth will be passed on to the congregations and religious communities who will bear the brunt of spiritually ill-formed leaders.

Moral Maturity

How does morality develop? Consider two very different options. In both, the focus is on how morality matures in a person, not the philosophical or theological argument about "the good" that is the goal of moral maturity.

When I was in graduate school, Lawrence Kohlberg's theory of moral development was the subject of a great deal of research and interest. He theorized that moral maturity is the result of growing through stages of moral reasoning. Like a young child who learns first to roll over, then crawl, then walk, then run, these stages are sequential. Development occurs as the individual moves from one stage to another. Individuals can use all stages of moral reasoning just as a child retains the ability to crawl after learning to run, but maturity is evidenced by the attainment of the more advanced stages of reasoning. The process that leads to these more advanced stages is a developmental one. The theory was not well supported by psychological research after Kohlberg's death, and its underpinnings have been roundly critiqued on grounds of philosophical and cultural analysis. But such critique invites a question: Does morality mature as a natural developmental process that is related (among other things) to the growth of cognitive ability?

Aristotle also had a model of how morality develops. He divided virtue into two kinds, virtue of the intellect and virtue of character, and argued that "Intellectual virtue owes its origin and development mainly to teaching, for which reason its attainment requires experience and time; virtue of character is the result of habituation."[13] By habituation, Aristotle meant "we become just by doing just actions, temperate by temperate actions, courageous by courageous actions." While nature gives human beings the ability to acquire virtues, nature does not produce them on its own. Nature may provide a muscle, in a sense, but the muscle becomes useful by repetitive actions that give it strength. Habituation or action, by itself, does not guarantee virtue. Aristotle argued that "by acting as we do in our dealings with other men, some of us become just, others, unjust; and by acting as we do in the face of danger, and by becoming habituated to feeling fear or confidence, some of us become courageous, others cowardly." Habituation is a necessary but not sufficient resource for developing virtue of character. Some thought is necessary to discern particular circumstances and to choose the right behavior. In a section on anger and spending money, for example, Aristotle wrote that "anyone can get angry or give and spend money— these are easy; but doing them in relation to the right person, in the right amount, at the right time, with the right aim in view, and in the right way—that is not [something] anyone can do, nor is it easy. That is why excellence in these things is rare, praiseworthy and noble."[14]

The structures that Aristotle had erected in antiquity Thomas Aquinas moved into a theological frame in the Middle Ages. Moral virtues are related to human "passions" or the affective aspect of being human. The cardinal moral virtues are prudence, justice, and courage, and because these virtues are related to passions, they require the crucial virtue of temperance. Aquinas thought, as did Aristotle, that these virtues mature by habituation—acts of temperance, for example, contribute to more temperance. The theological virtues—faith, hope, and love—come into being and mature in a human life in a very different way: they are gifts of God, "infused" by God. Aquinas writes that "virtue ordering man to a good as measured by divine law and not by human reason, cannot be caused by human acts whose principle is reason, but only by divine operation in us." Aquinas quotes Augustine in his explanation of theological virtues as virtues "which God works in us without us."[15] In this sense, the theological virtues mature more like spirituality, with all the indirection and ineffability that attend to growing spiritually. The moral virtues—prudence, justice, courage—mature with a combination of reason and habituation.

How does morality mature? Is it a form of human development process, as Kohlberg theorized? Or is it the result of instruction and habituation, as Aristotle and Aquinas argued? In the end, I think moral capacity matures more in the way that Aristotle and Aquinas argued than in the way Kohlberg argued, and the key for me is the combination of thought and behavior. While Kohlberg theorized that people will behave as their stage of moral reasoning instructs them to behave, I agree with Aristotle and Aquinas that moral understanding or virtue matures as a *combination* of reason and action and is influenced by teaching. Cultivating moral maturity in theological students requires helping them understand the morally right thing in a range of situations, which theological schools are pretty good at doing, and providing the setting and contexts in which they engage right action repetitively and over time, habituating the practice of the virtue, which schools are less good at doing.

If theological schools hope to contribute to moral maturity, they would do well to consider activities and structures that make it possible for students to engage in moral acts. Practices are already in place in some schools and can be put in place in others without huge institutional investment. These practices likely require rethinking the edges of theological education more than its center. Some practices may involve the incorporation of morally pregnant events that were not designed in the curriculum.

One of the more compelling stories in theological education occurred in 1960, when an African American student at Vanderbilt Divinity School, James Lawson, participated in civil rights activities and demonstrations. Most famously, he was in a sit-in at a lunch counter in downtown Nashville. He was arrested, and as a result the university board dismissed him as a student. That action prompted protests by students, divinity faculty, and other university faculty, and finally the trustees reinstated Lawson as a student at the divinity school.[16] I am sure that these events became the most morally educative moment in the lives of these divinity school students.

Other practices are built into the formal curriculum. The Meadville-Lombard Theological School revised its MDiv curriculum so that students experience their theological education through three broad contexts, one of which focuses on community analysis, social justice, and action. Each of the contexts raises moral issues, but this one in particular provides curricular engagement with social moral issues. Other practices occur alongside the formal curriculum. I was visiting with a group of seminary students there who were writing short letters or postcards to individuals working on issues of social justice. They gathered around a table with paper and addresses, stamps and envelopes, and spent an hour or two writing notes to encourage and thank people working on a range of justice and mercy initiatives. This was not part of a course or a classroom assignment, but their activity reflected what they had learned in class. Practices like this, along with the learning students receive in their courses, can contribute to the formation of moral maturity. As I have written more than once in this essay, many of the needed changes are revisions of what schools are already doing, or additions to it, rather than a restructuring of all their educational practices.

Relational Integrity

Just before beginning work on this chapter, I participated in a consultation called by an organization that works with congregations and pastors who are in conflict. These conflicts can be very painful for both church members and pastors, and as pressures on local congregations increase, it appears that these incidents are increasing. Members of the consultation discussed causes and possible strategies to employ to help pastors and congregations avoid these painful situations. Our discussion of causes centered on two areas. One was a fatal disagreement about expectations for the church, such as a community that had changed more than the congregation wanted to admit, or a pastor who had ideas that did not match the congregation's ethos or culture. The other was the inability of the pastor to relate warmly and effectively with members of the congregation—the pastor was aloof and hard to know, or given to anger, or insensitive to needs of others, or autocratic and demanding, or . . . the list goes on. In the 1970s study I mentioned earlier, thousands of laity and clergy rated qualities or characteristics of ministers and priests in terms of how important or detrimental they were for ministry. When these items were grouped into sets, the sets with the highest average ratings were "Service in Humility: Relying on God's grace, serves others without seeking personal reputation for success or infallibility"; "Personal Responsibility: honoring commitments by carrying out promises despite pressure to compromise"; and "Christian example: Personal belief in the gospel that manifests itself in generosity and a life of high moral quality."[17]

How can theological schools educate students so that they graduate with relational integrity? I think the effort begins with a critical examination of the role of personhood in ministry that attends to two different issues.

The first is the importance of relational integrity itself and the emotional health that it requires. Henri Nouwen wrote an influential book in the 1970s, *The Wounded Healer*, in which he noted the alienation and loneliness of modern people, including ministers; the declining status of ministry in the culture; and the resulting wounds that a minister often carries. Nouwen called upon ministers to make their own wounds "a source of healing." He did not mean that ministers should wear their wounds on their sleeves. "Open wounds stink," he wrote. The image of the wounded healer, however, seems to have taken hold more than the substance of his argument. Some students seem to think their wounds are evidence of personal honesty and even a qualification for ministry. Ministry requires healed wounds. Even at its best (and it is seldom at its best!), the work of ministry is emotionally taxing. It requires emotional health to survive and relational integrity to thrive.

The second issue that deserves attention is a recognition that relational integrity is not learned by hearing a good lecture on it, or by reading a good paper about it, or even by writing a personal reflection about it. To the extent that it is learned, it is learned in relational situations with others. As with moral maturity, one becomes relationally mature by relating. It helps to be able to reflect on why one related in a certain way with a particular person, and it helps to be coached in basic relational skills, but the reflecting and coaching are insufficient apart from the crucible of relating with people who are angry, withdrawn, manipulative, scared, distraught, bullying, insecure, uncaring, or warm and accepting. Theological education is rich with opportunities for students to encounter great ideas, holy ideas, and to develop a knowledge of God and the ways of God. It is not as rich with opportunities to mature relationally, although some are present.

Field or contextual education and clinical pastoral education (CPE) provide such opportunities. Field education was added to the curriculum as the professional model of theological education gained ascendancy in the twentieth century. Its primary focus was the development of professional skills. Like hospital rounds for medical students, contextual education was invented to provide real-time ministerial work under the supervision of an experienced minister, which in the best of circumstances is an excellent way to learn many pastoral practices. It also provides the most realistic arena for relating to people in a ministry context. The relational value can go unattended if field education instruction focuses on what was done and the way it was done without also addressing how students reacted to persons or settings the way they did. In formational theological education, the second kind of question is just as important as the first, and supervisors need training in how best to help students grow in relational ability as well as in ministerial skills. CPE developed in the twentieth century. Its hospital and institutional settings, especially when coupled with small-group meetings, provide relationally intense experiences. For many students, CPE's combination of a demanding ministerial setting, intense small groups, and skilled supervisors offers the most powerful formational experience for relational integrity that they have in theological education.

Schools seldom use another resource that is at their disposal, namely, careful screening of applicants. Not everyone with an undergraduate degree and a sense of call to or interest in ministry should be admitted. Some troubling relational tendencies may be present at the time students apply to seminary. Most schools, however, don't have in-person interviews with master's level applicants, and if they do, the interview is often more oriented to recruitment than to screening. The schools are not helped with their admission decisions when persons who recommend applicants do not raise concerns in their recommendation. Theological schools are also reticent to reject applicants because they really do believe in redemption: they admit even a student who clearly has difficulties on the assumption that the person will find relational redemption in the process of theological education. Relational integrity can be influenced by the right kind of educational engagement, but some human qualities are very durable and not amenable to change by the kinds of interventions a theological school can provide. A theological school's ultimate client is the communities of faith in which ministerial graduates serve, and if a school knows that someone has threatening relational qualities, it needs to serve its communities of faith rather than the aspirations of the individual applicant.

Christianity is a relational religion. It is a tradition in which adherents are called to love one another, and in which leaders need relational integrity. Like spiritual and moral maturity, relational integrity is something schools can nurture. Although they cannot create it, they must not ignore it.

Institutional Changes That Formational Theological Education Will Require

I have argued throughout this essay that formational theological education requires doing some of the same things schools have been doing in the way they have been doing them, doing other things they have been doing but changing their purpose or goal, and adding new things to what they are doing. In the end, this model of theological education will also require some institutional changes involving the evaluation of students, the organization of student learning, and the partners that theological schools engage.

CHAPTER 4

Evaluation

Schools have a long history of evaluating students. Most anyone who has ever gone to school has a story about evaluation—the grade that was unfair, the grade that was undeserved, the test that was ridiculously hard. Whatever form the evaluation took, students often remember it even after they have forgotten what they learned. Most of this evaluation is related to knowledge or skill, and schools develop rubrics—criteria by which a determination is made—for assigning a grade or other indicator of achievement. When I was in elementary school, I received grades for subjects like math, language arts, social studies, and science. But I got a mark (typically not a letter grade) for "conduct." After all, how much good behavior would be an A and how much bad behavior would be an F? Conduct was assessed differently than other subjects. But it was still assessed on the report card in elementary school because developing social skills is an important childhood task. Such assessments dropped away by high school as conduct problems were dealt with by correction, detention, or, in some cases, expulsion.

How should a seminary student's moral or spiritual maturity be evaluated? Is it more like an academic subject or childhood conduct? Should it be assessed with a grade, a mark, or some other instrument? Traditional patterns of evaluation might not fit something like spiritual growth. Theological schools that have courses on formation or spiritual growth often deal with the complexity by grading students either on a pass/fail basis (depending on whether they completed the work or not) or by some critical/constructive qualitative assessment of their spiritual growth. One way or another, if spiritual or moral maturity becomes a legitimate goal for theological education, some kind of evaluation of individual students will be necessary.

Formational theological education will require more attention to these more qualitative forms of evaluation. Schools will need to invent ways both to assess these qualities and to make that assessment count meaningfully in overall determination of the granting of a degree. If a degree cannot be withheld on the basis of failure to attain a reasonable level of spiritual or moral maturity or relational integrity, then these qualities would continue to be adjunctive to the "real" subjects of theological education, the ones that receive the "real" grades.

Other sectors of higher education employ evaluative strategies that differ from measuring achievement in knowledge or skill. Some PhD programs in clinical psychology, for example, make a determination about the emotional stability of students who will work as graduates in therapy settings with clients or patients. Advanced education in the performing and visual arts requires evaluation of not only skill and technique but also artistry and other less than objective qualities, and a jury of several people makes the judgment. Strategies like these could be employed to assess students' growth in relational ability or moral maturity. The more theological education attends to qualities of character and spiritual maturity, the more it will need to evaluate students by patterns that differ from default academic evaluation strategies.

Academic Disciplines

The most typical pattern of the organization of content in higher education is by disciplines, then subdisciplines, then by specialty within subdisciplines. As knowledge expands—as it does with great rapidity, even in the theological disciplines—more disciplines and subdisciplines develop. Disciplinary specialty is the primary way that faculty can claim expertise.

I was talking to a person who had recently been appointed to a seminary faculty and was attending a conference for new faculty members. I asked this talented individual, who had focused on the Pauline corpus in graduate school, what was most enjoyable about teaching in a seminary. He said the New Testament department at his seminary was large enough to allow a focus on teaching the Pauline literature. Disciplines are a wonderful way to organize ever-expanding information and provide a division of expertise and labor in a school, but in the day-to-day practices of ministry, they are not an effective way to organize information that graduates will need to lead communities of faith. Disciplinary structures simply do not fit the patterns of work for ministers and priests. They will teach and preach the Bible, for example, and even if someone took every course that faculty specialist in Pauline studies taught, he or she would still need to preach from the Gospels and other books of the New Testament, not to mention from the prophets, the law, and the history of the Hebrew Scriptures/Old Testament. Ministry doesn't occur in disciplinary units, and the distance between the structure of knowledge in ministry contexts and the structure of knowledge in the academy only increases as disciplines become more specialized.

The complex and necessary tasks of integration, which has primarily been the responsibility of the seminary student, need to become the responsibility of theological schools. Faculty need to do a major part of the integrative work, but that is contrary to the current intellectual moment's confidence in small pieces of information and suspicion about larger narratives that integrate them. The reasons for the suspicion are valid, as metanarratives are susceptible to the power of those who construct them, but the Christian faith makes most sense in the context of a metanarrative of creation, fall, redemption, and hope for the future. Formational theological education will need to attend to both specialized information of the theological disciplines and the construction of intellectually viable metanarratives that communities of faith will need in an increasingly secularized context. As with the evaluation of students, these intellectual needs of formational theological education separate the theological school from the conventions and intellectual moment in much of American higher education.

Engaging New Partners

A third adjustment that formational theological education will require is an increased engagement with new partners. Since the professional model matured in the middle of the twentieth century, theological schools have affirmed the value of field education and contextual learning. They have done so on a limited basis, however. Like law schools, they have tended to rely on the classroom or information-based educational strategies more than experiential learning contexts. For example, an 80-credit-hour seminary degree can be completed in many schools with only 6 credit hours of field education. If a credit hour assumes about 100 hours of experience, 6 credit hours amount to 600 hours of work in some ministry context. A master of social work degree, by contrast, involves fewer overall credit hours but 1,800 hours of supervised work in social work contexts. I mentioned earlier that relational integrity is nurtured by relational engagement. The limited value theological schools have tended to place on experiential learning will need to change. Formational theological education will require increased attention to the behavioral and affective learning that occurs in experiential contexts. It also will require a different kind of partnership among the theological school, the ministry contexts, and the mentors or supervisors who work with students. Partnerships exist in most schools, but they need to be multiplied in number and strengthened in depth. Supervisors also need to be given a more substantial role in evaluation of students. Cracks in relational ability, quickness to anger, or lapses in maintaining appropriate boundaries are more likely to occur in informal relationships among students than in more structured relationships with faculty. Ministry students are often better judges than faculty of the moral and spiritual maturity of students, and schools need to cultivate nonpunitive ways in which student feedback and evaluation are utilized to cultivate moral, spiritual, and relational growth. Formational theological education will require finding intentional ways to utilize and maximize the expertise, perceptions, and contributions of partners to accomplish its broad goals.

I have always been the kind of educator who is more interested in what to teach than how to teach, and likely I have scores of former students who can tell you about what that meant for their learning! I remain convinced that a teacher's most important pedagogical resource is knowing and loving the material being taught. Aristotle converted me to something more. For many ideas, it is only as the idea takes root in practice, as it is habituated, that its real intellectual substance takes form. Any goal of theological education is an irrelevant abstraction unless it has been learned, and learning requires perspectives, sensitivities, and strategies. I think that my uneasiness about pedagogical practice may be shared by other theological educators, and the result is a theological education that is less effective than it might otherwise be. Just as people cannot become more temperate without practicing temperance, theological educators need to practice being educators. Maybe I would have been a much more effective professor if I had paid more attention to Aristotle.

Formational theological education will require a careful assessment of educational practices. It will entail teaching some things theological schools have not always taught, teaching some things differently, and putting the spotlight on educational agendas that have been in the shadows. Formational theological education will require schools to consider their own vocation as schools, and for faculty to commit themselves to forms of faithfulness that embody the goals of formational theological education. It will require the commitments of institutions to formational theological education as an educational goal because it will cost more than the kind of education many are currently providing. The costs are not so much financial as they are connected to the way schools do things. Schools will need to learn how to do things they are not doing now, especially developing the institutional capacities needed to educate for moral and spiritual maturity and relational integrity. It will require some fundamental reorientation to higher education in general and several technical changes in the way degree programs are provided. The cost to the schools could be significant, but the cost for communities of faith and the future of Christian ministry if the schools fail to make these changes would be much, much higher.

Postlude

I originally began this extended essay by saying that I didn't want it to be personal, but when I tried to write it as if it were not, it didn't make sense. A great deal of mischief can come from an overly personal essay, but no other way to write seemed possible. Theological education has been my calling; it has also been a life that I have loved. I grew intellectually as a seminary student as much or more than I did in a PhD program. I cherished the years that I was a professor at a seminary working with students, and the years that I was an administrator at ATS working with presidents, deans, and faculty. The professional model of theological education I received was right for me personally and right for the church and its location in the culture. The forms and practices of theological education have been engaging and full of meaning for me. The proposal in this essay does not emerge from a sense that theological education is being done incorrectly or that something is broken and in need of repair. Theological education has been good for me and for the times.

If it was so good, why not continue it, update it with some improvements, and add more diversity in its practices? Does the next theological education need to be different from the last one? I have contended that historically theological education has been influenced by culture, by the church and religious practice, and by higher education. If these influential variables did not change, then theological education would not need to change. Maybe if even one or two remained the same, theological education would not need to change. As best I can tell, however, all three are changing.

The role of religion in American culture is changing. The week that I was drafting this postlude, the Religious News Service reported a recent National Opinion Research Center/Associated Press poll that shows that trust in clergy has continued to decline and that people, even some churchgoers, are not likely to consult clergy for a large number of important life issues like sexuality, finance, family planning, and medical or career decisions.[1] The number of persons who affiliate with religion in the United States continues to decline. The church has been one of the victims of the worst of priestly and ministerial behavior. The fastest-growing religious affiliation is "none." Few denominations have escaped the pressures of decline in membership and capacity. There are two houses of worship within two miles of where I live that have For Sale signs in front of them. Religious practices have changed a great deal since I entered seminary fifty years ago.

The character of higher education is changing. The denominational college that I attended, with its one thousand students and a basic liberal arts curriculum, is now a nondenominational teaching university with eight thousand students and a substantive focus on baccalaureate and graduate professional programs. In higher education in general, the sciences and technology have gained more academic prestige, while liberal arts and humanities have lost much of the prestige they once enjoyed. As admission rates at the most prestigious institutions continue to decline, other institutions are increasingly trying to find enough students to keep their schools going. Educational debt is soaring. Multiple public indicators suggest that higher education has lost its cultural luster; suspicions abound that its value may not be worth its cost. So much has changed that it would be reckless to assume that higher education has merely become an improved version of its 1969 self.

Society is becoming more secular and more polarized. Individuals are less influenced by traditional sources of authority, less likely to participate in social service organizations including church, and more likely to mediate social interactions through the Internet. When I began in ministry, the culture still extended a privilege to religion. It may have been undeserved, but it was present in both subtle and more obvious ways. Religion is still important in American life; the United States is the most religiously active liberal democracy in the world. Religious practices, participation, and presence in the culture, however, have changed.

I don't mean to paint a "sky-is-falling" picture. It is not. Many of these changes are neither for better nor for worse. Most are complex combinations of change in multiple directions. I proposed in the interlude after chapter 2 that these factors are powerful but not dictatorial. They call on schools to respond, to find the tune they need to sing in relationship to the dominant notes being sounded by influences they cannot change.

In a time when so much has changed and continues to change—a time that seems to be between the times—what should be the future of theological education? Some people want to get rid of all the furniture and start over, while others want to refinish a few pieces but otherwise keep everything just as it is. There is another option, and it is the one that I am proposing. It will seem too modest to some. Perhaps I am an old man trying to hold on to what has been so meaningful to me when it is no longer of use to anyone else. But maybe, just maybe, the task this time most requires is to go to the attic and retrieve some things that were put in storage because they were too valuable to give away. Their usefulness had not ceased, though their use had, for a time.

My proposal is to retrieve the qualities that the early church saw as crucial for its leaders—qualities that are never dated or go out of style—and then find ways to modify the goals and practices of theological education to focus on these characteristics. The future needs more theological education, not less. It needs all the study of text and tradition that the current model has provided, and it needs all the skills that are currently being taught and then some. But it needs more than that. It needs practices that cultivate moral maturity, relational integrity, and spiritual maturity, and when that is done well, it makes for a different kind of theological education. I have called it formational theological education. It is based on the hunch that the authority religious leaders in this new religious and cultural world will depend on is more the kind of Christian human beings they are than the professional competencies they possess. Professional capacities will be needed, of course, but they will not provide the authority for leadership they have provided in the past. Authority will accrue to leaders who have a deep identity as Christian human beings, who have life-centering religious commitments, whose moral and spiritual maturity demonstrate the presence of mature faith, and who possess relational integrity that reflects a faith in which God took on flesh to relate to the human family.

To provide the kind of theological education these kinds of religious leaders need, theological schools will have to change some of their educational and institutional practices. The way they educated students like me fifty years ago for intellectually viable knowledge of the tradition and skills for the practice of professional ministry will not be sufficient for religious leaders whose authority to lead will also require a deep, abiding, resilient, generative identity as Christian human beings.

I have often reflected on a line from *Little Gidding* in *Four Quartets*—even before it was listed in multiple websites of T. S. Eliot's "famous quotes" or published as a poster to hang on the office wall: "We shall not cease from exploration, and the end of all our exploring will be to arrive where we started and know the place for the first time." The ubiquity of the quotation does not negate its truth. It has been true for fifty years of seminary studies, work in ministry, teaching in a theological school, and serving the member schools of the Association of Theological Schools. As my career in theological education closes, I find myself simultaneously experiencing an old beginning and a new one. The old one is memory of the goodness of theological education as I experienced it, and the new one is a confident hope that the next theological education will be as right for its time as the last one was for my time. The goodness of the Christian faith has been worth a lifetime of labor, and it will be worth the labor of those who come after me.

For Further Thought

Each of the books in this Theological Education between the Times series includes a brief section for further thought. I have chosen to ask you two questions.

1. All politics, the saying goes, is personal. I don't know about politics, but the experience of both education and ministry is intensely personal. I have written this book with frequent references to my experiences, but if those references do the job they were intended to do, they will prompt you to think about *your* education in college or seminary or wherever.

   Who are the professors that most influenced you? What do you remember more about them: What they said, the assignments they required you to complete, or the kinds of persons they were and the way they treated others? What meaning might you draw from these memories?

2. During most of the years that I was a seminary professor, I asked students at the beginning of one course to think about the best minister they had ever known. I asked them to think of an individual, and then to write down the characteristics they associated with that person.

I would like you to do the same thing. Who is the best minister or priest you have ever known? What characteristics do you associate with this person?

Next, I would ask students to think of the worst minister they had ever known and write down the characteristics they associated with that person.

I would like you to do the same. Who is the worst minister or priest you have ever known, and what characteristics do you associate with that person?

After the students had written down the characteristics, I asked them to call out the words they had written, and I recorded them on the chalkboard (remember, I was a seminary professor many decades ago). Class after class, the results were similar.

Year after year, students identified the best ministers they had known by positive personal and spiritual qualities and the worst they had known by the absence of positive qualities or the presence of truly negative qualities. What do you think those students were saying about formational theological education? What do your responses tell you about formational education?

Notes

Chapter 1

1. Justo González, *The History of Theological Education* (Nashville: Abingdon, 2015).

2. Rudolf Bultmann, *Jesus and the Word*, trans. L. Smith and E. Lantero (New York: Scribner and Sons, 1958), 38.

3. Unless otherwise indicated, Scripture quotations come from the New Revised Standard Version.

4. Adapted from the standard for the MDiv, Association of Theological Schools in the United States and Canada, www.ats.edu/uploads/accrediting /documents/degree-program-standards.pdf. These accrediting standards were adopted in 1996 and were in force (revised) until 2020, when new accrediting standards were adopted.

5. Eliot Eisner, *The Educational Imagination: On the Evaluation and Design of School Programs* (New York: Macmillan, 1979), chap. 5.

Chapter 2

1. See Randall H. Balmer and Lauren F. Winner, *Protestantism in America* (New York: Columbia University Press, 2005).

2. Some of this material on mainline Protestant theological education is drawn from Daniel Aleshire, "First but Not Finished: Mainline Protestant Theological Education," in *Looking Forward with Hope: Reflections on the Present State and Future of Theological Education*, ed. Benjamin Valentin (Eugene, OR: Cascade, 2019).

3. Harvard University, https://www.harvard.edu/about-harvard/harvard-glance/history.

4. College of William and Mary, https://www.wm.edu/about/history/index.php.

5. Yale University, https://www.yale.edu/about-yale/traditions-history.

6. Glenn Miller, *Piety and Intellect: The Aims and Purposes of Ante-Bellum Theological Education* (Atlanta: Scholars Press, 1990), 48.

7. Margaret Bendroth, *A School of the Church: Andover Newton across Two Centuries* (Grand Rapids: Eerdmans, 2008), 15.

8. Miller, *Piety and Intellect*, 105.

9. American Historical Association, https://www.historians.org/about-aha-and-membership/aha-history-and-archives/brief-history-of-the-aha.

10. Phillip Hammond, *Religion and Personal Autonomy: The Third Disestablishment in America* (Columbia: University of South Carolina Press, 1992), chap. 1.

11. Abraham Flexner, *Medical Education in the United States and Canada Report: A Report to the Carnegie Foundation for Teaching* (New York: Carnegie Foundation for the Advancement of Teaching, 1910).

12. Robert Kelly, *Theological Education in America: A Study of One-Hundred Sixty-One Theological Schools in the United States and Canada* (New York: George H. Doran Co., 1924).

13. Joseph M. White, *The Diocesan Seminary in the United States: A History from the 1780s to the Present* (Notre Dame: University of Notre Dame Press, 1989), 29.

14. Christopher Kauffman, *Tradition and Transformation in Catholic Culture: The Priests of the Society of Saint Sulpice in the United States from 1791 to the Present* (New York: Macmillan, 1988), 10.

15. Kauffman, *Tradition and Transformation*, 39.

16. St. Mary's in Baltimore had an affiliated nonseminary program, but it was abandoned in the 1850s. The second seminary in the United States, Mount St. Mary's in Emmitsburg, did maintain a program apart from its seminary, and it is one of the few Catholic institutions that, from its founding, has maintained educational programs for priesthood candidates and for lay students.

17. See, for example, Julie Byrne, "Roman Catholics and Immigration in Nineteenth-Century America," National Humanities Center, n.d., http://nationalhumanitiescenter.org/tserve/nineteen/nkeyinfo/nromcath.htm.

18. White, *Diocesan Seminary*, 149–50.

19. White, *Diocesan Seminary*, 150, 157, 159.

20. Joseph White, "Leadership in the American Diocesan Seminary: Contexts, Institutions, and Personalities—1791 to 1965," *Theological Education* 32, supplement (1996): 39.

21. Society of Priests of Saint-Sulpice, https://www.sulpiciens.org/spip .php?article119.

22. "Decree on Priestly Training, *Optatam Totius*, Proclaimed by His Holiness Pope Paul VI on October 28, 1965," The Vatican, http:// www.vatican.va/archive/hist_councils/ii_vatican_council/documents /vat-ii_decree_19651028_optatam-totius_en.html.

23. The role of the minor seminary was continued in some high school seminaries, but only a few remain in operation.

24. Catholic population can be counted in two ways. The first is the number who self-report that they are Catholic in social surveys, and the second is the number who are actually connected to a parish. The second is the smaller and likely more accurate number of practicing Catholics and more closely parallels the number of adherents reported by Protestant denominations.

25. Statistics drawn from data published by the Center for the Applied Research in the Apostolate, Georgetown University, https://cara.georgetown .edu/frequently-requested-church-statistics.

26. *Program of Priestly Formation*, 5th ed. (Washington, DC: United States Conference of Catholic Bishops), 43 (hereafter *PPF*).

27. *PPF*, 30.

28. "The Causes and Context of Sexual Abuse of Minors by Catholic Priests in the United States, 1950–2010: A Report Presented to the United States Conference of Catholic Bishops by the John Jay College Research Team," United States Conference of Catholic Bishops, May 2011, http:// www.usccb.org/issues-and-action/child-and-youth-protection/upload/The -Causes-and-Context-of-Sexual-Abuse-of-Minors-by-Catholic-Priests-in-the -United-States-1950-2010.pdf.

29. Peter Steinfels, "The PA Grand Jury Report: Not What It Seems," *Commonweal*, January 25, 2019, https://www.commonwealmagazine.org /pa-grand-jury-report-not-what-it seems.

30. See Bill J. Leonard, "Southern Baptists and Evangelical Dissent," in *The Oxford History of Dissenting Protestant Traditions*, ed. Jehu J. Hanciles, vol. 4 (Oxford: Oxford University Press, 2019), 194 215.

31. James Davison Hunter, *Evangelicalism: The Coming Generation* (Chicago: University of Chicago Press, 1987), 5–6.

32. George Marsden, *Reforming Fundamentalism: Fuller Seminary and the New Evangelicalism* (Grand Rapids: Eerdmans, 1987).

33. Quoted in Virginia Brereton, *Training God's Army: The American Bible School, 1880–1940* (Bloomington: Indiana University Press, 1990), 55.

34. Quoted in Brereton, *Training God's Army*, 53.

35. All the dates listed with these schools are the dates of their initial accreditation by the ATS.

36. John Hannah, *An Uncommon Union: Dallas Theological Seminary and American Evangelism* (Grand Rapids: Zondervan, 2009), 53–66.

37. Chloe T. Sun has written about Logos Evangelical Seminary in her book in this series, *Attempt Great Things for God: Theological Education in Diaspora* (Grand Rapids: Eerdmans, 2020).

38. See Jackson Carroll et al., *Being There: Culture and Formation in Two Theological Schools* (New York: Oxford University Press, 1997).

39. Anthony Ruger and Chis Meinzer, "Through Trial and Tribulation: Financing Theological Education," *Auburn Reports*, 2014.

40. These data are drawn from respective lists of degree programs approved by the Commission on Accrediting for all accredited member schools of the Association of Theological Schools.

41. Timothy George, "The Baptist Tradition," in *Theological Education in the Evangelical Tradition*, ed. D. G. Hart and R. Albert Mohler (Grand Rapids: Baker Books, 1996), 39.

42. Mark Noll, *The Scandal of the Evangelical Mind* (Grand Rapids: Eerdmans, 1994), 12.

43. Noll, *Scandal*, 24.

44. Robert Putnam and David Campbell, *American Grace: How Religion Divides and Unites Us* (New York: Simon & Schuster, 2010), 105.

45. Robert Jones, *The End of White Christian America* (New York: Simon & Schuster, 2016), 53.

46. See, for example, Francis Fitzgerald, *The Evangelicals: The Struggle to Shape America* (New York: Simon & Schuster, 2017), and Molly Worthen, *Apostles of Reason: The Crisis of Authority in American Evangelicalism* (New York: Oxford University Press, 2014).

47. See, for example, Daniel Aleshire, "Gifts Differing: The Educational Value of Race and Ethnicity," *Theological Education* 45, no. 1 (2009): 1–18.

48. See the books in this series by Keri Day and Willie Jennings.

49. See Elizabeth Conde-Frazier's book in this series.

Chapter 3

1. See, once again, Robert Jones, *The End of White Christian America* (New York: Simon & Schuster, 2016).

2. ATS Commission on Accrediting 2018 Standards of Accreditation, www.ats.edu/uploads/accrediting/documents/general-institutional-standards.pdf.

3. Charles Foster et al., *Educating Clergy: Teaching Practices and Pastoral Imagination* (San Francisco: Jossey-Bass, 2006), 10.

4. Edward Farley, *Theologia* (Philadelphia: Fortress, 1983), 35.

5. David Kelsey, *To Understand God Truly: What's Theological about a Theological School?* (Louisville: Westminster John Knox, 1992), 34.

6. Farley, *Theologia*, 7.

7. Blaise Pascal, *Pensées*, trans. H. F. Stewart (New York: Modern Library, n.d.), para. 626.

8. Dan Stiver and Daniel Aleshire, "Mapping the Spiritual Journey," in *Becoming Christian: Dimensions of Spiritual Formation*, ed. Bill J. Leonard (Louisville: Westminster John Knox, 1990), 20.

9. The results of the original study were published in David Schuller, Merton Strommen, and Milo Brekke, *Ministry in America* (New York: Harper & Row, 1980).

10. Edward D. Hess and Katherine Ludwig, *Humility Is the New Smart: Rethinking Human Excellence in the Smart Machine Age* (Oakland, CA: Berrett-Koehler Publishers, 2017), 23.

11. David Kelsey, *Between Athens and Berlin: The Theological Education Debate* (Grand Rapids: Eerdmans, 1993, subsequently republished by Wipf and Stock).

12. James Burtchaell, CSC, *The Dying of the Light: The Disengagement of Colleges and Universities from Their Christian Churches* (Grand Rapids: Eerdmans, 1998).

13. Mark Schwehn, *Exiles from Eden: Religion and the Academic Vocation in America* (New York: Oxford University Press, 1993).

14. Douglas Henry and Michael Beaty, eds., *The Schooled Heart: Moral Formation in American Higher Education* (Waco, TX: Baylor University Press, 2007).

15. Council of Independent Colleges, https://www.cic.edu/programs/NetVUE.

16. Harvard University, https://gened.fas.harvard.edu/ethics-civics
-courses.

17. Karen Stiller, "Enthusiasts, Skeptics, and Cautious Explorers," *In Trust*, New Year 2019, http://www.intrust.org/Magazine/Issues/New-Year
-2019/Enthusiasts-skeptics-and-cautious-explorers.

18. Miroslav Volf and Matthew Croasman, *For the Life of the World: Theology That Makes a Difference*, chap. 5 with Justin Crisp (Grand Rapids: Brazos, 2019), 45, 61, 118, 120.

Chapter 4

1. Because I contend that Roman Catholic education for the ministerial priesthood is the most formational pattern of theological education, and am advocating formational patterns for all of theological education, and because the sexual abuse of minors by Roman Catholic priests is such a devastating issue in contemporary culture, the reader is reminded of the discussion of this issue in chapter 2.

2. The majority of ATS member schools participate in a questionnaire completed by incoming students. One of the questions asks new students to identify their primary motivations for pursuing theological study. In a list of almost eighteen options, year after year, students have rated "Experienced a call from God" most highly. (See table 18 in "Total School Profile," at Association of Theological Schools, November 16, 2018, https://www.ats.edu
/uploads/resources/student-data/documents/total-school-profiles/esq-total
-school-profile-2018-2019.pdf.)

3. See, for example, Mark D. Jordan's book in this series, *Transforming Fire: Imagining Christian Teaching* (Grand Rapids: Eerdmans, 2021).

4. Mark Schwehn, *Exiles from Eden: Religion and the Academic Vocation in America* (New York: Oxford University Press, 1993), 48.

5. Schwehn, *Exiles*, 49.

6. Schwehn, *Exiles*, 50–51.

7. Debbie Creamer, "Reimagining Assessment in Theological Education (via the Appalachian Trail)," *Theological Education* 52, no. 1 (2018): 51–61, https://www.ats.edu/uploads/resources/assessment/creamer-te-article.pdf.

8. See https://www.ats.edu/uploads/resources/assessment/roman-cath
olic-assessment-workbook-final%207-27-18.pdf.

9. See the entire primary instructional document on assessment at https://www.ats.edu/uploads/accrediting/documents/self-study-handbook
-chapter-7.pdf.

10. George Lindbeck, "Spiritual Formation and Theological Education," *Theological Education* 24, supplement (1988): 13.

11. Marvin Oxenham, *Character and Virtue in Theological Education* (Carlisle, UK: Langham Global Library, 2019), 30.

12. Hanan Alexander, *Reclaiming Goodness: Education and the Spiritual Quest* (Notre Dame: University of Notre Dame Press, 2001), 172.

13. Aristotle, *Nicomachean Ethics*, trans. Roger Crisp, rev. ed. (Cambridge: Cambridge University Press, 2000, 2014), 2.1, p. 23.

14. Aristotle, *Ethics* 2.9, p. 35.

15. Thomas Aquinas, *Treatise on the Virtues*, trans. John A. Oesterle (Notre Dame: University of Notre Dame Press, 1966, 1984).

16. The entire story is told in Dale Johnson, ed., *Vanderbilt Divinity School: Education, Contest, and Change* (Nashville: Vanderbilt University Press, 2001), see "The Lawson Affair, 1960."

17. David S. Schuller, Merton P. Strommen, and Milo Brekke, *Ministry in America* (New York: Harper & Row, 1980), chap. 4.

Postlude

1. Yonat Shimron, "New Poll Shows Growing View That Clergy Are Irrelevant," *Religious News Service*, July 16, 2019, https://religionnews.com/2019/07/16/new-poll-shows-growing-view-that-clergy-are-irrelevant.